SH*T
TOWNS OF
AUSTRALIA

RICK FURPHY & GEOFF RISSOLE

ALLEN&UNWIN
SYDNEY · MELBOURNE · AUCKLAND · LONDON

CONTENTS

INTRODUCTION

Australia is shit. Ever since it was invaded by Her Majesty's finest explorers and populated by her worst criminals, Australia has been a smorgasbord of shit towns—after all, shit people need shit places to live. The epic expanse of sundried excrement that simultaneously masquerades as a continent, an island and a country is sprinkled with a veritable fuck-tonne of crappy towns and shitty cities, from dusty desert shitholes to free-range bogan breeding grounds to megacities filled to the gunnels with highfalutin flogs. Surrounding this scattering of awful settlements is a vast country populated by the world's most dangerous creatures, from crocs and sharks to snakes and spiders, from drop bears and yowies to bin chickens and Tasmanians.

Shitting on towns is as much a national pastime as binge drinking or homoerotic ball sports. Ever since a syphilitic sea dog sailed into Botany Bay and declared the land to be completely empty (despite the presence of hundreds of thousands of Indigenous people for at least 50,000 years prior), Australians have revelled in taking the piss. This book sets out to inventory the diverse villages, hamlets and settlements that make up the 'Lucky Country', from the affluent to the effluent—the rural to the urinal—profiling all the best places not to visit or, heaven forbid, live.

The towns and cities reviewed in this volume have been carefully selected using an exacting set of scientific criteria developed at the prestigious University of Nimbin, combined with extensive field research and a healthy sense of humour. Some towns were so abjectly shit that we couldn't even summon a few hundred words to sum up their shitness.

Our research project has already made its mark on Australian society. Through our Facebook page we have received proverbial bags of fan mail from delighted residents all over the country, and we are pleased to share some of that correspondence in this book (names may have been changed). It's these kinds of messages that remind us every day why we do what we do.

Stay classy, Australia.
—Rick and Geoff

SIGNIFICANT EVENTS IN AUSTRALIAN HISTORY

65,000 BC	Aboriginal people discover Australia
3000 BC	The Egyptians discover Australia
1521	The Portuguese discover Australia
1550	Martians discover Australia (the first Australiens)
1606	The Dutch discover Australia
1681	The British discover Australia
1770	The British discover the rest of Australia and declare the land to be completely uninhabited, despite the presence of about half a million pesky natives
1788	The British begin shipping convicts to New South Wales, thus beginning the great Aussie tradition of establishing offshore detention centres in the Pacific
1824	The colony's name is officially changed from New Holland to 'Straya
1859	Australian Rules football is invented as an elaborate practical joke
1869	Australia remembers it has Indigenous people and starts nicking their children
1870	Ned Kelly pioneers the hipster look

1901	Australia plagiarises New Zealand's flag
1923	Vegemite is invented when yeast is accidentally mixed with wombat faeces
1932	Australia's military declares war on emus, and loses
1953	Bob Hawke sets a new world record for skolling a yardie, which remains the single greatest achievement by an Australian
1960	Future anti-boat people PM Tony Abbott arrives in Australia by boat
1967	PM Harold Holt is eaten by a water dingo
1973	The White Australia policy is abolished as Australia starts pretending it's not racist
1979	The release of *Mad Max*, a famous documentary about Australia
1985	Rolf Harris presents the child abuse prevention video *Kids Can Say No! (But I Hope They Don't)*
2006	Steve Irwin is assassinated by the animal kingdom
2013	Swino the pig drinks three six-packs of beer and fights a cow
2015	Tony Abbott munches an onion like it's an apple, inadvertently revealing his reptilian nature
2016	A pig called Apples and a kangaroo called Fuck It begin a sexual relationship

HOW TO SPEAK AUSTRALIAN

Communicating with an Australian can be a challenging experience. Unlike other notoriously difficult to learn languages like Esperanto or Klingon, Australian doesn't follow an easily discernible pattern. Below are a few simple words and phrases that will help you navigate your travels in the Lucky Country.

MATE	friend
MATE	enemy, villain
MATE	lover
MATE	complete stranger
CUNT	friend
CUNT	enemy, villain
CUNT	lover
CUNT	complete stranger
THONGS	flip-flops
ICE	meth
PISS	beer
VB	piss
BOWSER	petrol pump
SERVO	petrol station
BOTTLE-O	liquor store

TRAINO	train station
ARVO	afternoon
HOMO	homeowner
BARNEY	fight
BIFFO	fight
STOUSH	fight
BLUE	fight
FRIENDLY CHAT	fight
STREWTH	???
BANTER	racism
POOFTER	university graduate
GLASSING	Australian handshake
LARRIKIN	person in need of serious psychiatric help
UN-AUSTRALIAN	Aboriginal, immigrant or woman
I GO FOR COLLINGWOOD	my parents are related
AFL IS THE BEST CODE	sometimes I just need to feel another man's strength inside me
I VOTE FOR ONE NATION	I sat too close to the microwave as a child
IF THEY ARE GENUINE REFUGEES THEY SHOULD FOLLOW THE RULES	I have an inverted penis

TEN
SIGNS YOU
LIVE IN A
SHIT TOWN

1. Your New Year's fireworks display consists of setting a stolen car on fire

2. The most famous person to come from your town is an animal

3. The only tourists who visit are due to a Google Maps error

4. You still have a video store

5. The only 'ethnic' restaurant in town is a kebab shop

6. The only time your town was on TV was in a documentary about missing backpackers

7. You voted for the Nationals

8. The only things of value ever produced by your town are asbestos and some guy who got two correct answers on *Who Wants to be a Millionaire?*

9. You regularly leave the house in pyjamas

10. You live in Queensland

QUEENSLAND

Famous for heat, cyclones, obesity and racism, Queensland is the Australian version of the American Deep South minus the culture, where everyone drinks XXXX and wears XXXL. Also known as 'cane toads' or 'banana benders', notoriously insular Queenslanders are easy to provoke—don't make eye contact or it will be interpreted as either an invitation to fight or a mating ritual. The state's tourism slogan is 'Beautiful One Day, Perfect the Next' but 'Shit One Day, Completely Fucked the Next' would be more accurate.

Cairns

Cairns was inexplicably built on a swamp in uninhabitable Far North Queensland, making it a sweltering shitbox with a million per cent humidity year-round. The city experiences two seasons: the wet season, featuring an unrelenting torrent of rain and tropical cyclones, and the even wetter season. Temperatures range from far too hot to face-melting. Even taking a dip won't cool you off as the water is frequently warm enough to boil a baby. Nevertheless, the punishing heat forces many poor bastards to brave the water, presenting them with the choice of cavorting with crocs and box jellyfish in the sea or paddling between toddler turds and blobs of backpacker jizz in 'The Lagoon'.

Despite featuring a climate unsuitable for human life, Cairns has managed to leverage its proximity to the bleached remains of the Great Barrier Reef into a thriving international tourism industry, which means the town is now lousy with heat-stricken backpackers rooting in public, fighting in the street and getting high from Gatorade bottle bongs. Other popular tourist activities include being the victim of car theft, getting mauled by psychotic cassowaries and being left stranded in the middle of the ocean by a Great Barrier Reef dive tour. Cairns's most iconic landmark is a humungous statue of Captain Cook giving a Nazi salute in a nod to Australia's race relations record.

TOWN SLOGAN We Don't Know How to Pronounce it Either!

FAN MAIL

What goat rooting take it up the fuck wit
wrote this. **(DIGBY GUNT, CAIRNS)**

Written by some shit for brains from inner Melbourne
god one Fuk wit! **(BARBARA CHODEWORTH, TOWNSVILLE)**

Maybe your one of those fucked up vegans that
don't have brains, idiot. **(LUSLEY PLORP, MOUNT ISA)**

Shit towns of Australia, you suck. No longer following you're
page and I suggest everyone else do the same. Whoever
the admin is needs to stick their head up their own bum
and have a look around. Tossers. **(DIEGO FREECLUG, MOUNT ISA)**

Townsville

Townsville (or Towntown in English) was named after Robert Towns, a notorious slave trader who was well known for the practice of 'blackbirding', which is Australian for abducting Pacific Islanders and forcing them to work on your sugar cane plantations. In true shit town fashion, Townsville honoured its namesake with a bronze statue for his services to racism.

Townsville has been dubbed the unofficial capital of the 'Tropical North', complete with all the horror that entails: oppressive heat, nightmarish disease and wildlife that devours wayward tourists. And that's just Flinders Street on a Friday night. Also nicknamed 'Brownsville' due to its arid climate rather than the complexion of its residents, Townsville has an annual rainfall comparable to the dustier parts of the Sahara, aside from the handful of days when it's pelted with the sort of biblical monsoons that would get Noah's arsehole twitching.

Townsville also has an impressive collection of defunct sports teams, including the A-League's Northern Fury Football Club (who were not very angry and only vaguely played football) and the Townsville Crocodiles basketball team (who managed a staggering zero titles in a largely mediocre 23 seasons). The pride of Townsville is the North Queensland Cowboys, who are best known for getting thumped by the Broncos and fingered by John Hopoate.

ALSO KNOWN AS Brownsville, Clownsville, Drownsville.

MOST FAMOUS PERSON Julian Assange, international hide-and-seek champion 2012–19.

Mackay

Like its northerly neighbour Townsville, Mackay is also named after a slave lord, suffers from asphyxiating humidity and is populated by the sort of feral Queenslanders that even Brisbane won't put up with. Controversy abounds over Mackay's location for administrative purposes as neither North Queensland nor Central Queensland wants it.

Built off the back of slave labour, the most prominent industry in Mackay is sugar, with the city showing an impressive commitment to morbid obesity and adult onset diabetes. Mackay was named Australia's Fattest City in 2018, with a massive 83 per cent of adults overweight or obese, the most exciting thing to happen to Mackay since an outbreak of the bubonic plague in 1918. Sugar is so treasured in Mackay that it's often cut with cocaine to pad it out.

Aside from producing a product responsible for most of the lifestyle diseases in the developed world, Mackay's other main industries are mining, tourism and making fraudulent cyclone insurance claims. Mackay serves as a gateway to the Great Barrier Reef and Whitsunday Islands, ironically at the same time as fuelling these natural wonders' destruction (and the severity and frequency of the city's cyclones and floods) by selling vast amounts of coal to overseas global-warming factories. A popular tourist activity is whale watching, the common term for observing people from Mackay. If you're itching to put yourself in a sugar coma in a tropical setting, visit 'Fat Townsville' today!

Mount Isa

Mercifully tucked away in the middle of buttfuck nowhere, Mount Isa is a toxic desert hellscape with a lengthy rap sheet of shitness. The city revolves around its lead and copper smelters, belching pollution plants that provide work to the local population of deadset drongos and foolhardy FIFOs, as well as furnishing them with a free citywide sulphuric fart fragrance and bonus lead poisoning. Having babies with learning disabilities and third arms is all part of the job for the hardworking lead-heads of 'The Isa'.

Another part of the job is embracing the oppressive heat of Mount Isa, a place so parched that even the so-called 'wet' season is dustier than the Parramatta Eels' trophy cabinet. The influx of men to work in the mines has also turned the town into a veritable sausage fest, to the point where in 2008 the mayor actually suggested ugly women come to Mount Isa to get laid. Unfortunately for anyone keen on taking up His Worship's offer, the lead smelter has rendered most of the male population impotent—or, ironically, lacking lead in their pencils.

When they're not busily poisoning the planet, Mount Isans enjoy getting on the goon, fighting in the street, pelting cars with rocks and harassing backpackers at the Irish Club. Mount Isa's smog-soaked sunrise can be a spectacular sight—if you ignore the silhouettes of shopkeepers hosing human shit off the footpath. The city's premier event is its combined rodeo and mardi gras every

August, when LGBTQ people are chased down the main street by enraged bulls.

As a result of the local death factory turning a bunch of bog-standard yobbos into a pack of CUBs (Cashed-Up Bogans), inhabitants of Mount Eyesore pay through the arse for the privilege of living in such a pootopia. Everything is exorbitant, from the price of drowning your sorrows at the local pub to the cost of escaping—a flight to Brisbane can set you back more than flying from Brissie to London. On the other hand, whatever it costs, it's worth it.

TOWN SLOGAN	Happiness is Mount Isa in Your Rear-view Mirror.
ALSO KNOWN AS	The Isa, Mount Ice-a, Mount Arsa, Mount Eyesore, Mount Isalation, Mount Isis.
MOST FAMOUS PERSON	Lindy 'A Dingo Ate My Baby' Chamberlain.

Rockhampton

Reluctantly settled by a bunch of stranded miners, Rockhampton soon became known as 'The City of the Three S's' (sin, sweat and sorrow). The slogan survives to this day, except now it stands for slobs, steers and semen.

The city is also known as the 'Beef Capital of Australia', a reference to its plethora of fast-food outlets and morbidly obese population. Rocking 'Rocky tuxedos' (extra-wide jeans and XXXL flannos), Rockhampton's blubbery bogans are celebrated by a giant sculpture of a dugong and seven Big Bull statues. Sadly, the bulls have all had steel rods rammed through their nut sacks in an effort to end the local tradition of getting blind drunk on shit beer at a leagues club and nicking a Big Bull's ball. Rockhampton capitalises on its Beef Capital moniker by selling overpriced supermarket steaks to gullible tourists who couldn't tell a Scotch fillet from a Scotch egg.

Shoved 40 kilometres up the Fitzroy River, Rockhampton is also known for its unbearably humid climate, giving it its third nickname, 'Australia's Sweaty Armpit'. In summer, the oppressive humidity combines with the dank stench of the river to create a truly revolting miasma. The city gets so hot that taking a dip in a crocodile-infested swimming hole seems like a good idea.

Even the city's streetlights agree that the city is a horror show, clearly spelling out 'HELL' when viewed from atop Mount Archer. A little-known fact is that town planners were actually trying to write

'HELP', in a desperate plea to passing aircraft to rescue them from living in Rockhampton.

ALSO KNOWN AS Rocky, Rock Vegas, Hampo, Rockhammer, Rockdumpton, Freakhampton, Cockhampton, Crackhampton, Shithampton, Hell.

DID YOU KNOW? People from Rockhampton are known as 'Rock Spiders'.

FAN MAIL

The answer is simple, if you don't like , Sex and travel. (Fuck off). **(VIGO PASTRY, BUNDABERG)**

you don't know SHIT for brains some joke my arse it's dam right insulting the arsole who wrote this trash doesn't even deserve a comment on it how dare anyone knock OUR coastal resorts. **(THORALD OXYMORON, SUNSHINE COAST)**

You don't like it FUCK OFF YOU DICK HEAD GO AND DO CPR ON YOUR DADS COCK CUNT. **(MERIDIAN FAP, BRISBANE)**

FAN MAIL

sum1 should report this pleb ...go have
another wank **(ALDRIN BREAKFAST, IPSWICH)**

Get the fuck. Go back where ya from. Fucken
assholes. **(KODAK BROOMYDAY, LOGAN)**

The gc is better then most places in nz or you
wouldn't all be chopping at the bit to come here!!!
Stay in nz with the dreads of society is you's
all fit right in. **(BARTON CHUMKO, GOLD COAST)**

Bundaberg

Named after photogenic necrophiliac Ted Bundy, Bundaberg is famous for rum, macadamia nuts and unemployment—but mainly rum. The city is essentially alcoholism with a postcode. In fact, 'Bottleoberg' is such a booze-soaked alcohopolis that its premier tourist attraction is a giant rum bottle, which is popular among tourists who enjoy taking selfies of themselves dry-rooting it for an edgy new Tinder pic, and locals who are still trying to figure out how to open it to get the grog out. Another popular attraction in the area is the Mystery Craters, 35 unexplained holes in the ground, or 36 if you include Bundaberg.

Despite a thriving grog industry, Bundaburgers somehow manage to drink more booze than they make, which may explain Bundy's sky-high rate of violent crime and nation-leading number of dole bludgers. Popular pastimes in Boganberg include drink-driving down the main strip in a stolen Holden, doing drunken skids down 'The Hummock', and bashing backpackers for not being from Australia. Like most of Queensland, Bundaberg is prone to heavy flooding, but all the floods seem to do is momentarily sober up the local population before they dry everything off and get back on the piss.

ALSO KNOWN AS Bundy, Boganberg, Blunderburg, Chunderburg.

MOST FAMOUS PERSON Herbert Hinkler, the first person to fly solo from England to Australia. As the pioneer of the great Aussie gap year, he presumably returned with alcohol poisoning and several new STDs.

Fraser Island

Loitering with intent off the coast of Queensland, Fraser Island is a swampy lump of sand that doubles as an overpriced, overrated tourist trap. Hundreds of thousands visit the world's largest sand island each year to fry in the sun, shit in the dunes, jizz in the lakes or be mauled by a dingo in its natural habitat. Another popular reason for visiting Fraser is by accident after crashing a boat into it.

As well as rusty shipwrecks, a series of large puddles and rainforests teetering precariously on top of sand dunes, Fraser features a resident population of mangy flea-bitten dingoes, venomous snakes and seasonal saltwater crocs. Fences to deter dingoes are commonplace because they keep eating tourists, while dogs are banned from the island because they keep rooting the dingoes. Fraser is also home to a couple of hundred humans, about the same number of residents as your average housing commission home in Mount Druitt.

Fraser Island was originally named 'Great Sandy Island' but had to change its name because while it is exceptionally sandy, it is definitely not great. The former Aboriginal internment camp is the perfect place for a holiday you'll regret forever.

ALSO KNOWN AS Razor Island.

Sunshine Coast

The Sunshine Coast is a slightly less awful version of the Gold Coast, but that's like comparing a shit sandwich with a diarrhoea taco. While the Gold Coast is famous for roller-coasters, failed sports franchises and STDs, the Sunshine Coast is known for cranky boomers, a complete lack of nightlife and a painful line-up of 'attractions' that are somehow less fun than staying at home. It's essentially the Gold Coast for people who are confused by flashing lights.

From Maroochydump to Poosa Heads, the Sunshine Coast is a cluster of bulging shit towns clinging to the coast like septic haemorrhoids, populated largely by geriatrics wanting to die somewhere sandy and warm. Hobbies include whingeing about the Gold Coast, reminiscing on the days when the Sunshine Coast was cow-pat-covered paddocks before the tourists and developers ruined everything with all their money and First-World facilities, and getting stuck on the Bruce Highway trying to escape to somewhere less horrible.

For visitors, the Sunshine Coast has everything required for a disappointing holiday. The area's main family attraction is a theme park dedicated to the national culture, featuring such controversial rides as the Coward Punch Coaster, the Drink-Drive Dodgems and the Racism-Go-Round. Another drawcard is the Buderim Ginger Factory, which produces an estimated 40 per cent of the world's undesirable babies. The factory has a number of ginger-themed rides including the Ginger Train, which also happens to be the name of a popular activity in the homosexual community. Confusingly, the Buderim Ginger Factory is no longer located at Buderim, having moved to nearby Yandina in 1980 without bothering to change its name.

The Sunshine Coast is also home to an excessive number of Australia's embarrassing 'Big Things', including the Big Pineapple at Woombye, the Big Pelican at Noosaville, the Big Mower at Beerwah and the Big Crack Pipe at Nambour. The only redeemable feature on the Sunshine Coast is its beaches, at least until they are swallowed by rising sea levels, taking the region's entire economy down with them. On the plus side, by the time climate change really kicks into gear, the entire population of the Sunshine Coast will have already succumbed to death by old age.

ALSO KNOWN AS Scumshine Coast, Suncrime Coast.

Caboolture

Sitting on top of Brisbane like a sweaty arse on a toilet seat, Caboolture is a nightmarish mish-mash of deros and rednecks, a feral hellhole that is arguably more Logan than Logan. Cabo's population exploded when Brisbane evicted its housos, New Zealanders and other undesirables before the World Expo 88, causing the once sleepy hamlet of Caboolture to devolve into a slum of epic proportions. As unplanned as most of its pregnancies, the town is now an ungroomed patch of urban pubes sprouting around a haggard highway and crawling with the lice of society.

Caboolture is the nation's capital of welfare fraud, animal cruelty and playing pokies in your pyjamas. Other common hobbies include blowing up gelignite at sportsgrounds for shits and giggles, fishing up a body from a waterway, or doing a shoey on Toohey. The home town of Keith Urban hosts an annual country music festival and 'ute muster', attracting inbreds and simpletons from across the state. Aside from Urban, Cabo's biggest celebrities are the 'Centrelink Cougar', a middle-aged woman accused of seducing teenagers for their welfare money, and 'Bottles', a young lady famous for sticking bottles up herself at the Morayfield skatepark each weekend.

ALSO KNOWN AS Cabo, Capoolture, Cabullshit, Staboolture, Kabulture.

Brisbane

A sprawling subtropical shitburbia, 'Brisvegas' is a notorious cultural graveyard where high art is spray painting dicks on walls and fine dining is choosing not to use the drive-thru. The city manages the neat trick of combining small town attitudes with the crime and congestion of a major city, so is a great destination if you are in the mood to get mugged at knifepoint while being told to fuck off back to where you came from.

As well as being brain-achingly boring, Brisbane is prone to flooding and hot as buggery. The city spends a significant amount of time underwater yet always seems to be in drought. The heat is so oppressive that it makes residents do a whole range of irrational things, like casual racism and supporting the Broncos. Other popular pastimes include queueing up to suck off the Wally Lewis statue outside Suncorp or getting coward punched in Caxton Street by a moron in maroon. Brisbane is also overrun by all manner of pests including foxes, bats and New Zealanders.

Despite being known as 'The River City', Brisbane is in fact bisected by a dirty brown trickle that is more Missi-shitty than Mississippi. The river is recommended to anyone who gets off on gawking at a sludgy smear that looks like something on a men's room wall. Crossing the 'Brown Snake' by car requires taking out a second mortgage to pay the hefty tolls on the imaginatively named Go Between Bridge. Brisvegans are also strangely proud of their beaches, despite the

nearest being nearly two hours away in crippling traffic. The only strip of sand within the city limits is Streets Beach, a nasty man-made slurry pit full of used condoms and dead bin chickens. Another source of misplaced local pride is Brisbane-brewed XXXX, so named because Queenslanders can't spell beer.

TOWN SLOGAN The BrisBane of Australia's Existence.

ALSO KNOWN AS Brissie, Brisvegas, Brisvegarse, Brisneyland, Jizzbin, Brisbinchicken.

MOST FAMOUS PEOPLE Brisbane is a fountain of terrible music, responsible for such aural atrocities as the Bee Gees, Powderfinger and Savage Garden.

TEN THINGS TO DO IN BRISBANE

1. Get beaten up outside a Broncos game

2. Do a spot of dogging up Mount Coot-tha

3. Get mauled by an ibis at South Bank

4. Float down the Brisbane River in an upturned wheelie bin

5. Get bitten by a mosquito with Ross River virus

6. Get a mother–daughter two-for-one in Fortitude Valley

7. Get trampled trying to get a show bag at the Ekka

8. Watch your house be devoured by termites

9. Shout 'Queenslander' at someone minding their own business

10. Get confused by the concept of daylight saving

Toowoomba

Few people actually know where Toowoomba is and even fewer have ever been there. The regional city was strategically placed just close enough to Brisbane for Brisbanites to dump their unwanted elderly but far enough away that they don't have to visit them. Consequently, Toowoomba is full of xenophobic old people and stuffy God-botherers who are less into beaches and bitches and more about gardens and golliwogs.

Toowoomba's name is derived from the fact that widespread incest has resulted in large numbers of local women sporting multiple sets of genitals (or 'two wombs'). Popular alternative names include 'Double Douchehole' and 'Multi Minge'. People from Toowoomba are officially known as Toowoombarbarians, Toowoombastards or Toowoompaloompas.

As well as being a gulag for geriatrics, Toowoomba is known as 'The Garden City' because a few patches of manicured scrub are the closest thing it has to a point of interest. The highlight of the city's calendar is the annual Carnival of Flowers, when nannas from across the nation take time out from knitting things no one will ever wear, spouting nonsense on talkback radio and soiling themselves to pore over plants' private parts. Due in part to excessive gardening, Toowoomba is rapidly running out of water, which will come as a relief to most residents considering how it tastes.

Disturbingly, gentrification has begun turning Toowoomba into the Melbourne of Queensland, with graffitied laneways, scungy alley cafes and moustachioed vegans popping up with increasing frequency. The city is being invaded by so much diversity that long-time Toowoompaloompas are struggling to know who to fear anymore. The only certainty is that Toowoomba will always find a way to stay shit.

ALSO KNOWN AS T-Bar, Poowoomba, Twoheadwoomba, The Woomb, Double Douchehole, Multi Minge.

MOST FAMOUS PEOPLE Famous Toowoompaloompas include elderly pirate Geoffrey Rush and motorsports driver Will Power, who apparently stole his name from a self-help book.

Ipswich

Brisbane's grotty basement, the shitellite city of Ipswich is a notorious breeding ground for a whole range of unsavoury types, including dole bludgers, drug addicts and NRL players. Most of Ipswich's residents live in vast shanty towns surrounding Centrelink, whiling away the days until their next handout drinking homebrewed liquor, getting their area code tattooed on their neck, playing darts with used syringes and impregnating teenagers. The city's pride and joy is the annual Ipswich Festival, five days of free family entertainment including a stolen car parade, an arson display and a race riot.

Ipswich is perhaps best-known as the home town of Pauline Hanson, who parlayed a background in deep-frying battered cod into a political career pandering to racist rednecks who think that asylum seekers are fleeing war zones in leaky fishing boats so they can nick their jobs. In many ways Pauline Hanson is Ipswich personified—unsightly, predominantly government-funded, and full of shit. The only useful thing she has done is be great fodder for a hate wank. Ipswich continues its tradition of defective politicians by churning out an endless line of corrupt councillors, which would be remarkable if mayors being jailed and entire councils being sacked weren't commonplace in Queensland.

Ipswich's shambolic governance is reflected in the state of the joint, the only city in Australia that is literally a dump. Tonnes of trash is trucked in from across Queensland and New South Wales nightly and poured into old mines and empty lots in Ipswich, drenching entire neighbourhoods in a horrendous stench as well as smoke when the flammable stuff catches fire. On the plus side, the mountains of garbage do match the local decor of mould-coated houses and snake-infested abandoned cars adorning front lawns.

Two of Ipswich's finest alumni were a pair of rooted units who made a golf ball bomb, left it in the street and blew off a kid's hands. One of the dipshits later blew off his own hands as well as parts of his genitals in a separate incident. Clearly, the only hope of salvation for Ipshit is the Bremer's banks bursting during one of the city's frequent floods and washing away the bogans in a biblical deluge.

ALSO KNOWN AS Ippy, the Switch, Iphole, Ipshit, Shitswich, Icewich, Dipswich.

Logan

There's a reason Logan rhymes with 'bogan'. Fittingly, it also rhymes with 'grogan', 'Paul Hogan' and 'crime-infested war zone'. Logan's reputation as a bogan nest is so prevalent that the local council spent millions of dollars on a campaign to change the city's image—unfortunately, they spent it all on ugg boots and a container load of RTDs.

Appropriately named after one of Australia's most loathed colonial commanders, Logan is sandwiched between Brisbane and the Gold Coast, making it ideally placed to catch the human dregs of both cities. Its population comprises a motley crew of yobbos, drongos, housos, druggos and immigrants who thought they were moving to Brisbane. Logan is one of Australia's most diverse cities—in fact, it has more STD strains than the entire cast of *Goldie Shore* combined.

Common hobbies in Logan include getting shitfaced and hitting someone with a bit of wood, committing ram raids in hot-wired Holden Colorados, and intergenerational welfare dependency. A popular venue is the Logan Hyperdome, where flannel-clad rednecks fight to the death over Centrelink payments.

Logan's standout suburbs are Slacks Creek and Woodridge, twin slums that host all the panelbeaters, payday lenders, pawn shops and pokies you can menacingly shake a stick at. These suburban hellscapes are also ideal locations for the procurement of illicit substances, with more shoes on powerlines than on feet.

Gold Coast

The Gold Coast fancies itself as Australia's version of Las Vegas, which is true because it's a tacky tourist trap adorned with fake tits, a shit casino and an unending parade of timeshare presentations. The cluster of hotels masquerading as a city is where Australia keeps its unemployed Kiwi scaffolders while they wait for their shot at a third-rate reality show, and has-been strippers with multiple children to multiple men from multiple outlaw motorcycle gangs. If you are looking to get a shit neo-tribal tattoo or contract some novel form of super chlamydia, then the Gold Coast is probably your place!

Given that it's Australia's entertainment capital, the Gold Coast is filled with a plethora of such options, with the only downside being that they are all tacky and shit. On the Gold Coast, fine dining is 'all-you-can-eat pancakes' and a fun day out with the family features theme parks with worse safety standards than a Malaysian airliner. Popular staples of Gold Coast nightlife include visiting a vampire-themed cabaret staffed entirely by people who look like they recently failed HIV tests, getting attacked by a lower grade league player with 'roid rage', or being thrown off a balcony after a Tinder date gone wrong. A popular event on the Gold Coast is 'Schoolies Week', which gives high school kids the chance to experiment with alcohol poisoning and tradies from Logan the chance to experiment with getting passed-out high school girls into the back of their van.

The Gold Coast hosted the 2018 edition of the Commonwealth

Games, an event that used to exist only so Britain's former colonies could see who had the fastest slaves and now only exists to give white people who are too shit for the Olympics the chance to win medals, making it the Caucasian Special Olympics. The event celebrated the city's rich sporting history, which includes multiple failed professional franchises across at least three sports.

ALSO KNOWN AS Goldie, Cold Ghost, Dole Coast.

MOST FAMOUS PERSON The 'Candyman', a failed former AFL player and current tobacco mogul who whiles away his days hosting million-dollar orgies and shagging a bevy of porn stars, making him so Australian he should probably replace the emu on the coat of arms.

TEN THINGS TO DO ON THE GOLD COAST

1. Spend a day stuck in traffic on the M1

2. Buy a pair of thongs from a vending machine

3. See a famous beach before it erodes away

4. Get rescued from a rip by a cunt in budgie smugglers

5. Get trampled by a stampede of pelicans at Labrador

6. Get scammed into buying a timeshare

7. Watch a sports game in an empty stadium

8. Get mauled by a bull shark in a canal

9. Snort a line off a Meter Maid's arse

10. Get drunk enough to fight a Samoan bouncer

NEW SOUTH WALES

Named after the most inbred of the Home Countries and colonised by the first wave of convicts to land in the Lucky Country, New South Wales is now the most populous state in Australia. From the megaplopolis of Sydney to anonymous rural dungheaps, New South Wales features a diverse array of shit towns housing many different types of dickhead. The state's official sport is discussing house prices and its official sexual position is crying under the doona.

Nimbin

If you're venturing through northern New South Wales and see a sign welcoming you to Nimbin, run for the surrounding hills. The anarchic enclave is inhabited by feral packs of cannibalistic anti-vaxxer chemtrail conspiracy theorist mountain hippies, to whom local law enforcers have long since conceded defeat. You can identify these dangerous creatures by their retina-burning tie-dye shirts, knee-length dreadlocks and made-in-China Tibetan hats. Do not engage with the Nimbinese, do not share their weed, and whatever you do, do not purchase their tacky T-shirts or home-crocheted bong cosies—this will only encourage them to peddle more pointless crap and discourage them from having a shower and getting a job.

The permanently stoned citizens of the country's cannabis capital can seem initially charming, but things will quickly take a sinister turn if you get too close to a Nimrod—it's all too common for naive tourists to wander into an innocent-looking drum circle only to find some waster with the munchies munching on their leg. Remember, if bitten by a Nimbinian, you too will become a Nimbinian and will soon be overwhelmed by an insatiable lust for human flesh and an irrational urge to play with devil sticks.

The most perilous times to visit Nimbin are during the annual MardiGrass festival, when droves of hippies descend from their mountain hideaways to smoke inhuman amounts of weed in public, or during the Nimbin Roots Fest, which is the same thing but with music.

FAN MAIL

All the shit he says is conspiracy and not happening is actually whats really happening ... If you dont like reality being shoved in your face watch the fake media tv and newspapers ful of elite agendas stab yourself and those you love with toxins and dna altering substances ignore the obvious weather modification programmes or fluoridated water or the chemtrails. sheep stay in packs. **(SUNLEAF MOONFLOWER, NIMBIN)**

Love that priceless compared to hipster wankers. In Melbourne. City full brain dead. Idiots. Who working in jobs. Woch. Tv. Like a current affres. Footy. Get dunk on satday night. Who vote liberals ore alp. Nice see dumping on. People. Who can think. Creative. People. So if find hippys. Want unverty. in sydiny and Melbourne. Quite the city. For nimbian. Artist and musician. How ned hear ther thoughts. Work out rat races. What I dick head. **(MARJORIE CHODEWIDTH, NIMBIN)**

Byron Bay

Renowned as Australia's easternmost point, Byron Bay is also the country's biggest dickhead magnet. Every type of fuckwit under the sun gravitates to Byron: smelly hippies spilling out of their housevans, tattooed surfers fighting each other for territory, barefoot bogans fighting each other for fun, cashed-up boomers flittering between overpriced organic cafes and bullshit galleries, and overseas millionaires buying up the entire town for holiday homes. It's the sort of place that corporate shills on their second divorce fantasise about moving to so they can open a yoga retreat and root a dreadlocked barista on the beach. Byron Bay is Disneyland for dropouts, or the Gold Coast for people who prefer their Meter Maids to have hairy pits.

Overrun by tourists and littered with their half-eaten takeaways and used condoms, the only people who actually live in Byron Bay are pretentious trustafarians who turned up for Splendour in the Grass and forgot to fuck off home after the mushies wore off. These private school plastic hippies use their old man's money to live the 'Byron dream' and subsidise their supposed 'free spirit lifestyle', which actually consists of wearing cheap jewellery they bought in Bali while complaining about other fake hippies, catching herpes from German backpackers and generally doing large amounts of serious fuck-all. Byron Bay gained national notoriety for rejecting fast food giants McDonald's and KFC under the pretence that junk food didn't fit with the 'Byron lifestyle'—maybe if Macca's started serving kombucha and lentils and giving away hacky sacks in their Happy Meals it might have got the Byron seal of approval.

Byron Bay is known for its nightlife, which consists of drunken drongos and schoolies smashing each other's teeth out and projectile vomiting at passers-by. It's also a prime spot for spotting whales, which is why Byronites were still slaughtering humpbacks as recently as the 1960s. A popular feature is the Cape Byron Lighthouse, which serves the vital purpose of warning passing seafarers away from the complete wankeropolis of Byron Bay. We suggest you heed its warning.

ALSO KNOWN AS Moron Bay.

MOST FAMOUS PERSON Chris Hemsworth owns a giant fortress at Byron, where he goes to escape the pressures of being paid millions of dollars to dress up as a superhero.

TEN THINGS TO DO IN BYRON BAY

1. Catch crabs from a deadlocked surfer

2. Get a hand job during a drum circle

3. Learn erotic macramé

4. Overpay for a shit tipple

5. Get shat on by a German backpacker

6. Prolapse your anus while attempting an advanced yoga move

7. Get your chakra cleansed by a recent divorcee

8. Shelve a healing crystal

9. Get third-degree burns in a fire-juggling accident

10. Become a certified master of reiki healing by completing a two-hour online course

Lismore

Wedged between attention hogs Byron Bay and Nimbin, Lismore is the forgotten middle child, the central link in a human centipede, the anus between two butt cheeks. It's the DUFF (Designated Ugly Fat Friend) of the Northern Rivers, a town whose sole purpose is to make its neighbours look good by comparison.

Built in a big hole on the site of a destroyed rainforest, Lismore is a subtropical shitbox prone to frequent flooding, earning it the nickname Atlantismore. Lismore locals, or Lismorons, are an eclectic collective of undesirables: 'artists' (dole bludgers), 'alternative lifestylers' (meth cooks), 'freethinkers' (cult members) and dropouts who couldn't be buggered making it all the way to Byron Bay.

Lismore employs several cunning tricks to ward off stray visitors, including a plethora of hippie galleries selling bullshit, a network of porous roads punctured by potholes large enough to swallow cars, and an army of pointless sculptures that the council commissioned instead of fixing the roads. Natural tourist detractions range from the disgusting weed-choked Wilsons River to the disgusting shallow swamp that was once Lismore Lake. The city's proudest feature is a big log called the Big Log. If you have time, try to avoid them all.

ALSO KNOWN AS The Wok, Lizardville, Lisbore, Liswhore, Jizzmore, Shitmore.

MOST FAMOUS PERSON The generic pub rock band Grinspoon, who are only fondly remembered by people who got a hand job in a portaloo at the Big Day Out while 'Chemical Heart' played.

Casino

The Northern Rivers shithole of Casino is called that despite the fact that the closest it gets to an actual casino is the pokies at the RSM club, making it the most misleadingly named town since Woodenbong or Bigtitti. In an ironic twist, Casino has actually been banned by the New South Wales government from acquiring any more gaming machines. The town is more accurately known for cows—Casino claims to be the country's 'Beef Capital', or 'the Rockhampton of Australia'. In fact, Casino has such a boner for beef that it is considering changing its name to Cowsino.

Casino celebrates its beef fetish in three major ways: by regularly filling the town with the fragrance of rancid offal from its local meatworks; by legally restricting all food in the town to meat pies; and by holding an annual Beef Week, which attracts bloodthirsty bogans from all over the immediate area. Casino Beef Week, which is actually twelve days long because Casinoans don't know what a week is, features events such as the Beef Queen pageant for the most bovinesque lady, an orgy of animal abuse called a 'rodeo', and an orchestrated stampede of cows down the main street before a parade runs directly over all the fresh cow shit.

While in Casino, it's highly likely that you'll be approached by local bums begging for booze or meth money, but don't give them any—they'll only spend it on beef.

FAN MAIL

Shame yah mother mated with a goanna and had you shit town. **(BASIL CENSUS, GRAFTON)**

Coffs are actually friendly and nite people you STUPID CUNT! **(RHONDA DREDGE, COFFS HARBOUR)**

Hey dopey it was Korffs harbour named after a sea ferring Caption. **(BERTIE CHODES, COFFS HARBOUR)**

This is unaustralian and your an arse. **(NORMAN ESPERANTO, PORT MACQUARIE)**

Grafton

Grafton was founded by self-proclaimed 'cedar-getters' and originally named 'The Settlement', suggesting the city's founding fathers possessed the combined vocabulary of a learning-impaired toddler or the 45th president of the United States. Today, Grafton is best-known for its two dominant features: a gaol in the middle of town that ought to house all who surround it, and a double-decker deathtrap of a bridge with notorious hair-raising corners at each end. The bendy bastard links the deserted CBD with the slum named South Grafton and is appropriately accessed via Bent Street.

Grafton is populated by a variety of unsavoury types, including junkies making bumpers from gutter butts, rednecks writing country songs about fisting horses, and hoons doing doughies in their 'show cars' in between impregnating their underage girlfriends. The local league team goes by the name the Grafton Ghosts, presumably because they get killed in every match.

Grafton hosts an annual Jacaranda Festival dedicated to its favourite type of tree, which is the world's weakest excuse for a half-day piss-up. Another half-day off not working is awarded for the Grafton Cup, which is like the Melbourne Cup but with shitfaced deros in wife beaters and league shorts instead of shitfaced deros in thousand-dollar suits. The most exciting thing that happens in G-Hole is when the bull-shark-infested Clarence River floods every few years.

Coffs Harbour

Coffs Harbour is synonymous with bananas, blueberries and bulldogs. The city's most famous feature is the Big Banana Fun Park, a B-grade family attraction built around a giant phallic fruit sculpture and showcasing all the fun things you can do with a banana, at least two of which are appropriate for children. Other sad attractions include a marine mammal slave camp and the Clog Barn, which celebrates everything about Holland except the fun stuff.

'Coffs Harbour' is a misspelling of 'Coughs Harbour', so named because the town's entire settler population had smallpox. Consequently they were shunned by their neighbouring settlements, causing a profound hostility that persists to this day. Coffs Harbourians are some of the most unfriendly, arrogant and judgemental bastards one could have the misfortune to meet. They are fiercely proud of their city, despite it lacking any points of interest beyond a big yellow dong, a highway with 700 sets of traffic lights, an NRL scandal and a legacy of birth defects from toxic pesticides. Coffs is a comatose beachside ghetto and cultural wasteland with nothing to do but truckloads of meth. Indeed, it might be the only place where there are no jobs but everyone still judges you for not having one. The only thing going for Coffs Harbour is that no NRL team will ever hold a Mad Monday there again.

TOWN SLOGAN Far Coff!

ALSO KNOWN AS Coffs, Cough Harder, Cops Harbour, Cocks Harbour, Bananatown.

MOST FAMOUS PERSON Russell Crowe owns a sprawling estate just outside Coffs Harbour and often staggers barefoot into town to drown a few pints and growl out a couple of Cold Chisel covers.

Armidale

Armidale is known as 'New England' because it actually has four seasons, a novelty in Australia. Unfortunately, three of those seasons are winter, when the city is pelted with gargantuan hailstones and blanketed in a haze of toxic smoke from wood burners.

Aside from its shit climate, Armidale is known for its shit university, the sort of uni that people who can't get into proper uni go to, a third-rate diploma mill churning out unemployable graduates in nonsense subjects like basket-weaving and Australian history. The majority of students make the sensible decision to study by distance learning to spare themselves the indignity of actually setting foot in Armidump.

Armidale's prime selling point is its long and boring history. The main street is called Beardy Street, named for two of the founding settlers who had large beards, a fitting tribute to a pair of proud pioneering women. The city is awash with heritage buildings, though their aesthetic is slightly tarnished by the chicken wire encasing the balconies to prevent Armidallos from biffing beer bottles at passersby. Armidale also hosts the annual Australian Wool Fashion Awards, which showcases the season's hottest beanies, socks and garish jumpers, attracting nannas from across the nation. There are no entertainment options for normal people.

ALSO KNOWN AS New England, Dramadale, Farmidale, Harmidale, Armifail, Scumidale, Arsedale, Armihole, Armidump, Armidangerous, Armedrobbery.

FAN MAIL

I will bet that you live in some poofter place like
Sydney or Melbourne, so just go and get fucked from
me and my dog's.. **(PAVLOVA GONAD, BROKEN HILL)**

Obviously another "educated dick head" with
2 dicks, cos he couldn't get that silly playing
with one! **(SOLOMON DINGLEBERRY, DUBBO)**

What a heap of shit. You've lied to the public. Typical
ignorant Sydney journalists. You should work at the
daily telegraph. **(GLORIA RINGBARK, NEWCASTLE)**

You's a all full of SHIT. **(RON MEXICO, GOSFORD)**

Tamworth

Tamworth's main industry involves accumulating more nicknames than your average aggressively hetero Aussie white bloke. It's the 'First Town of Lights' because it was the first place in Australia to use electric streetlights. Unfortunately for the residents of Tamworth, that's where the technological progress stopped. It's also known as the 'National Equine Capital of Australia' due to locals' insatiable lust for horsemeat.

The town's most famous moniker is the 'Country Music Capital of Australia', a sobriquet celebrated with an annual country music festival that sees hillbillies from as far afield as Dubbo congregate to listen to punishing ballads about broken-down utes and unfaithful sheilas. The highlight of the festival is a Shannon Noll impersonator doing doughies in a Holden Colorado in the car park of Big W while chugging a schooner of Tooheys New.

Tamworth fancies itself as Australia's version of Nashville but has not managed to produce any musicians of any real note, with its primary export being staff-fucker and closet New Zealander Barnaby Joyce. However, Tamworth does at least rival its American sister city at incest, with most residents closely related on both sides of the family. Caution is highly advised before embarking on a wild evening of webbed-foot square dancing with the opposite sex in Tamworth.

Tamworth's landmarks include a giant golden guitar to mark the town's fondness for terrible music, and until recently a humungous sculpture of a Big Mac next to a war memorial. A popular tourist attraction is Tamworth Marsupial Park where punters can get up close with some of Australia's weird native creatures, which is really great if you've been harbouring a secret desire to touch a wombat.

If you're absolutely itching to hear a shitty cover of a Slim Dusty tune while munching a Phar Lap sandwich and getting a six-fingered handy, Tamworth is your town.

ALSO KNOWN AS Tammy, Scumworth.

Port Macquarie

Named after an autocratic governor with a penchant for massacring Aboriginal people and stealing their children, Port Macquarie was founded as a brutal penal settlement before becoming a prison for old people waiting to die. The seaside snorefest is overrun with two of Australia's biggest pests: koalas and the elderly, two demographics known for their low energy levels, weak eyesight and disgusting mating habits. When they aren't going to town on a gum tree or indulging in some casual racism, Port Macquarie's inmates are fond of doing serious fuck-all. If New York is 'The City that Never Sleeps', Port Macquarie is 'The City that Barely Stays Awake'. In fact, boredom has been legally mandated in the town to avoid overstimulating the locals. Port Macquarie has been named the least affordable smaller city in Australia, although the income stats are somewhat skewed because everyone is either retired or a marsupial.

Port Macquarie's main visitor attraction is the Hello Koalas Sculpture Trail, where tourists can peruse over 60 individually hand-painted statues of chlamydia-riddled four-thumbed freaks. If you'd prefer to surround yourself with leathery geriatrics whipping out their wrinkly bits, opt for a day at a local beach. Otherwise, there are always the time-honoured tourist favourites of running all the way home while screaming or driving your rental car off the nearest cliff.

TOWN SLOGAN The City that Sleeps.

Broken Hill

More of a shanty town than a city, Broken Hill is a bunch of decaying buildings clustered around a slag heap on the edge of the outback. The 'Broken' in its name comes from the fact that the entire place is a mining-depleted toxic wasteland, from the boarded-up shops and abandoned mines to the corrugated iron shacks that pass as dwellings, to the undrinkable drinking water, to the playgrounds coated in poisonous lead dust. Even the hill after which the town is named is long gone. Broken Hill has a pace of life so slow that if it were a person it would have been switched off a long time ago. The only businesses still operating are a phenomenal number of pubs—in fact, Broken Hill's official motto is 'Our drinking town has a mining problem'.

Despite being located in New South Wales, Broken Hill is actually closer to Adelaide than Sydney, a fate most people wouldn't wish on their worst enemy. However, geography is irrelevant to the uneducated and solipsistic inhabitants of Broken Hill, who live in a state of blissful ignorance of the outside world, simply referring to everywhere else as 'away'. Broken Hillbillies are so befuddled that they even observe the wrong state's time.

Broken Hill is famous for 'cheese slaw', an unholy melange of cheddar, carrot and emu semen that only the most depraved individuals would claim is food. The city's proudest points of interest are the Big Ant (a truly disappointing spectacle), the Big Bench (a totally impractical seating arrangement) and the Living Desert Sculptures (a series of sandstone chunks surrounded by a fuck-tonne of nothing). The region served as the principal filming location for *Mad Max 2*, making use of its post-apocalyptic landscape and resident tribes of feral bogans and motorcycling gimps. The local community radio station is called 2Dry FM, a dual reference to the dusty shithole's desert climate and lack of a sustainable water source. Broken Hill is less FIFO and more FIROITNSITNTBSA (Fly In, Run Out Into The Night Screaming In Terror Never To Be Seen Again).

ALSO KNOWN AS The Yabba, Busted Mound, Broken Hell, Broken Hole, Bogan Hill, Brokeback Hill, Grogan Hill, Scrotum Hill, Broke 'n' Ill.

DID YOU KNOW? The official language of Broken Hill is Broken English.

Dubbo

Dubbo is well known for its open-range zoo, exhibiting such species as lions, critically endangered elephants and rhinos, and the common red-necked wallaby. Dubbo is also well-known as an open-range zoo, exhibiting such species as dole bludgers, juvenile delinquents, critically endangered law-abiding citizens, and the common rednecked Australian. These creatures can be observed in their natural habitat rampaging up Macquarie Street shoplifting and vandalising vehicles, or pelting posties with rocks and bottles in 'Wild' West Dubbo.

Similar to the breeding program run at Dubbo's drive-thru zoo, the town itself runs an informal inbreeding program, making do with its isolation-enforced shallow gene pool in typical rural New South Wales style. Dubbo's proclivity for incest is just one possible explanation for its inhabitants' antisocial tendencies.

Other than visiting the zoo, entertainment options in Dubbo include paddling through mounds of rubbish in the filthy Macquarie River, or cycling up the slopes of Dubbo in 40-degree heat while being chased by violent children brandishing homemade spears. Most tourists leave either bitterly underwhelmed or in an ambulance after being stabbed by a five-year-old.

ALSO KNOWN AS Dubvegas, Grubbo, Dumbo.

DID YOU KNOW? Dubbo is home to a genre of EDM known as 'Dubbo-step', characterised by a bassline built on the rhythmic sound of a couple of meth fiends rooting in a McDonald's toilet stall.

Newcastle

Founded as a dumping ground for Britain's most dangerous convicts, Newcastle's notoriety as a godforsaken shithole still lingers two centuries later. Named after Newcastle in England, New South Wales' second-largest settlement has done its best to replicate its namesake's reputation as a depressing post-industrial hellscape famous for its aggressive locals, impenetrable local dialect and crap football team. The city's inmates pretentiously refer to themselves as 'Novocastrians', despite the fact that none of them can spell it.

Newcastle's main industries are filling the atmosphere with toxic smog, pillaging the earth and complaining about people from Sydney. 'The Steel City' is so fond of its working-class image that even its footy team wears hi-vis. The only things that emit more smoke than the stacks are the droves of deros lining the CBD accosting passers-by for a durry.

Despite its blue-collar reputation, Newcastle is propped up by a plethora of public service jobs, making it less of a 'bogan Pittsburgh' and more of a 'sooty Canberra'. Other Novocastrations include surfers (stoners), musos (junkies) and footy jocks ('roiders), all decked out in 'Newcastle sports coats' (jizz-stained flannelette shirts).

Newcastle is exceptionally proud of its NRL team the Knights, despite the fact that they haven't made the finals since 2013 (or roughly six prime ministers ago). In addition to their impressive collection of wooden spoons, the club is most famous for almost going

bust after being bought by a bogan billionaire, while their best player is mostly known for doing enough pingers to kill a whole wisdom of wombats.

Until recently Newcastle's biggest attraction was a massive penis-shaped tower, which the council demolished out of sheer embarrassment in 2018. The city now has nothing to promote other than the rusted carcass of a port with a decrepit CBD welded on, rows of abandoned shops and the country's biggest KFC. Hunter Street Mall and Marketown are popular bashing hotspots, while Fort Scratchley and Strzelecki Lookout are where most Novocumstains are conceived.

TOWN SLOGAN NSW's Number Two!

ALSO KNOWN AS The Steel City, Newy, Poocastle, Spewcastle, Screwcastle, NukedArsehole.

MOST FAMOUS PEOPLE Silverchair, a shitty Nirvana cover band from the nineties.

Central Coast

Combining featureless urban sprawl with some truly degenerate savagery, New South Wales' Central Coast is a rat king of shit towns. Boasting such attractions as syringe-littered beaches, copious roundabouts and shit roads, the area houses a diverse array of arseholes including tourists, old people, thugs, human seagulls and people who work in Sydney but couldn't bring themselves to live in Sydney.

The poo in the Cenny Coast's crown is Gosford (short for 'Godforsaken Hellhole'), the area's derelict CBD. Full of deros, druggos and dole bludgers, the epitomical shit town is commonly referred to as 'Mount Druitt by the Sea', 'Sandy Parramatta' or 'Nautical Campbelltown'. Popular activities in Gosford include asking strangers for cigarettes, spray painting your name on a train or keeping your pants up with a length of electrical cord.

'Gosford' is also slang for a particularly short skirt, as the town is close to a holiday resort called The Entrance. Appropriately, gosfords are the standard dress choice of the town's carefree female folk, usually paired with a thin strip of fabric as a top and no underwear, while the blokes favour Tapout shirts tight enough to show off the fruits of their disciplined steroid abuse.

Gosford is home to the Central Coast Mariners football team, who play their home games at three-quarters of a stadium on the waterfront. Due to a dearth of fans, the ground only has stands on three sides; the fourth borders a road by the sea, allowing the Mariners' usually wayward strikers to boot the ball into the drink with unsurprising regularity.

Other crapholes along the Coast include 'Terrible' Terrigal, 'Wrong' Wyong, and the activewear-wearing single-parent mecca Copacabana (named after a Barry Manilow song). The Entrance magically transforms into the Gaza Strip annually after being ravaged by Sydneysiders over the Christmas period. The witticisms 'God's waiting room' and 'the world's only above-ground cemetery' have been co-opted to describe numerous retirement towns but were originally coined by Spike Milligan for the geriatric camp of Woy Woy, a sort of mini-Gosford but with even more coffin dodgers.

Whether you are an old fart wanting to expire by the ocean or simply feel like getting stabbed at a beach, the Central Coast is for you!

ALSO KNOWN AS Cenny Coast, Centrelink Coast, Mental Coast.

Orange

Australia's most ungoogleable place, Orange is an utter waste of space famous for just about everything except oranges, with the only problem being that all of its claims to fame are about as impressive as a pair of soiled undies. While Orange is clearly a terrible name for a town, it's not quite as terrible as its original name, Blackman's Swamp. The city was initially named after an early settler, but following outrage from inner-city lefties it was renamed to honour a Dutch religious extremist.

Orange is known for producing a range of fruit including apples, pears and grapes. It is far too cold in Orange to grow oranges. The name is at least appropriate in another sense as Orange is home to a staggering number of rangas, which the city celebrates with an annual Ginger Pride festival. Conveniently, this event is scheduled for 31 October, which allows it to double as Halloween for normal people who are rightly terrified by masses of gingernuts.

Aside from fruit and firecrotches, Orange is also renowned for its thoroughly unpleasant winters which make it the snowiest city in the country, the amount of snow rivalled only by the amount of ice. Meth-heads and morons are as bountiful as apples in Orange, with torching stolen cars doubling as a popular pastime and the only way to stay warm.

For those not of a ginger or criminal persuasion, there are no attractions or entertainment options in Orange. Disappointingly, the city has squandered the opportunity to erect a giant novelty orange on the main road through town, an unforgivable and frankly un-Australian oversight. Googling 'things to do in Orange' returns the result 'Did you mean: things to do with an orange', which turns up some very disturbing images. Adding a 'NSW' results in 'Did you mean: things to do in Bathurst'. Orange you glad you don't live in Orange?

TOWN SLOGAN Orange is the new Blackman's Swamp.

DID YOU KNOW? Orange is one of four Australian towns that share their names with fruit, along with Berry in New South Wales, Banana in Queensland and Uglifruit in Tasmania.

Bathurst

Bathurst exists for one reason only: as the location of the Bathurst 1000, otherwise known as Bogan Christmas. This annual orgy of car carnage sees vast hordes of mechanophiles drink-drive from as far afield as Logan, Geelong and Greater Western Sydney for a long weekend of cheering on their favourite international automobile manufacturing conglomerate. It's Australia's version of the Gathering of the Juggalos but somehow even more white trash, *The Hunger Games* for people with mullets and meth mouth.

In an effort to reduce the booze-fuelled anarchy, authorities have imposed a limit of one box of grog per drongo per day, barely enough to keep the average Australian male awake. Enterprising yobbos have taken to burying crates of VB months prior to the Great Race and digging them up on the big day in the most bogan treasure hunt possible. Popular side events include blowing up toilet blocks, firebombing ice-cream trucks and pissing in the middle of Kings Parade.

Bathurst makes several dubious claims to fame, usually related to its long and boring history, in an attempt to pretend that it's not just a car race town. Locals are quick to point out that it was the site of Australia's first gold discovery, was the first European settlement on the western side of the Great Dividing Range, and holds the Guinness World Record for the most cars with ridiculous mods, racist bumper stickers and alcohol ignition interlocks. Bathurst's main permanent tourist attraction is the National Motor Racing Museum, a museum for people who don't go to museums. The city is also renowned for its remarkably low average intelligence, a combined effect of its elevation and excessive petrol fumes.

Bathurst may be known for its burnout-scarred racetrack but its best road leads directly out of this petrol-soaked tyre fire of a town.

ALSO KNOWN AS Crashhurst, Smashhurst, Bashhurst.

Lithgow

Cold, grey and stranded in the Blue Mountains, Lithgow is deader than a baby in a dingo's den. The miserable ghost town is inhabited by packs of listless mountain people with pallid skin and dead eyes, all permanently adorned in trackpants, otherwise known as 'trackie daks' or 'sex offender trousers'. The only daytime activities in town are sitting around, watching tumbleweeds roll down the main street and staring at people, while 'nightlife' consists of sitting around, getting smashed on cheap piss, watching the odd drag race down the main street and staring at people. If you do plan to visit, be warned that cracking a smile in Lithgow will get you beaten up.

Lithgow's industry consists of numerous mines, mills, plants and factories all closing down as fast as they can. The only things still operating there are a train station that does a roaring trade on departures and a maximum-security prison. Lithgow was the site of the Small Arms Factory, a weapons plant manned entirely by people with small arms. The factory went belly-up when it became clear that its genetically challenged workers were significantly less productive than their competitors.

Lithgow's premier event is the annual Ironfest festival, which includes a jousting tournament and a colonial war re-enactment, attracting virgins from all over New South Wales. A popular nearby attraction is the Glowworm Tunnel, which is popular mainly because it provides visitors with an excuse to briefly leave Lithgow. The disused

railway tunnel is filled with glowing lights which are mistakenly
believed to be glowworms but are actually the illuminated eyes
of Lithgow locals lurking in the shadows and staring at tourists. In
Lithgow, it's not just the bracing cold that will give you shivers.

ALSO KNOWN AS Liffgow.

Penrith

A bunker of blue-collar (or no-collar) bogans at the base of the Blue Mountains, Penrith is a super-slum notorious for its population of feral housos, yobbos and other ruffians. Despite the loose nature of its inmates, the Greater Western Sydney suburb is actually replete with amenities that any westie can truly appreciate: bespoke meth labs, palatial pokie dens and loads of wilderness in which to hide a body. The Penrith uniform consists of a mullet or rat's tail, ugg boots and a flannel shirt with a pack of Winnie Blues tucked into the upper sleeve (unisex) with a Southern Cross tattoo on either the bicep (for men) or the right breast (for women). The most popular pastime involves proud Aussie primary school dropouts moaning that they can barely make their next meth payment because educated immigrants took all the jobs.

Penrith is commonly known by locals as 'Penriff' or 'The Riff' due to the local accent/speech impediment, a source of constant confusion for Sydneysiders passing through on their way to Liffgow or Baffurst. The suburb's most popular sports team is the Penrith Panthers, or in local parlance, the 'Panfers'. The NRL team originally carried the derisive nickname 'the Chocolate Soldiers', which interestingly, given the make-up of their fan base, was not a racist slur but actually a reference to their shit-coloured jerseys.

Penrith is also home to the Museum of Fire, a tribute to the suburb's long tradition of urban arson.

whats wrong with snow you dickheads
(MINGUS IGLOO, ORANGE)

Who wrote this shirt **(GARFIELD GOLDSWORTHY, ORANGE)**

Do you have a brain or did you catch the idiot bus
to Stupidville. **(MERVYN TINGLE, WOLLONGONG)**

You are a ankle mate,2 foot lower than a
c***. **(CARMELLA SOOKWELL, WAGGA WAGGA)**

dis iz h8 speak m8 **(TOMOTHY GRONK, SYDNEY)**

Sick of all this picking on the west. You wouldn't write
about Sydney city you coward. **(GULLIVER PAPPS, PENRITH)**

Sydney

Otherwise known as 'London for Aussies who can't handle a twenty-hour flight', Sydney is a sweltering shit crucible beset by a confusing layout, horrific traffic and ever-increasing property prices that mean the only people who can really afford to live there are crooked investment bankers, crooked politicians and the children of crooked media moguls.

Sydney's iconic landmarks are the Sydney Opera House (which was designed by a Dane), Sydney Harbour Bridge (which was designed by Scots) and Bondi Beach (which was nicked from the natives). In addition to Bondi, Sydney boasts an abundance of beaches, which would be great if not for the fact that most of its residents spend the majority of their time either working to pay outsized rent or mortgages or stuck in seemingly endless traffic jams. If you do find five minutes to visit a beach, it will be covered with tourists and Instagram models scrapping to take the perfect selfie. Nightlife is no longer an option after 'Sadney' implemented nonsensical lockout laws designed to curb Australia's favourite nocturnal pastime: coward punching strangers while queuing for a dodgy kebab.

In many respects Sydney is actually a bunch of shit towns loosely amalgamated into a giant, sloppy, steaming shitropolis. The eastern suburbs are filled with ex-private-school boys driving midlife crisis machines, looking for their next trophy wife while avoiding being charged with insider trading. The northern beaches are filled with surfer stereotypes who refuse to cross the bridge under any circumstances and will happily stab you for the perfect wave. The inner west is filled with paleo-obsessed hipsters supping on a wide range of soy-based beverages while pursuing a career as a 'social media influencer' and letting their property developer parents pay their rent. Southern Sydney is where flag-wearing rednecks stage most of their race riots. While the majority of Sydneysiders like to pretend their city ends somewhere around Annandale, Greater Western Sydney is where they keep their bogans, benefit cheats and prospective ISIS recruits.

ALSO KNOWN AS Sydders, Sydneyside, Sadney, Shitney, Sydenee.

TEN THINGS TO DO IN SYDNEY

1. Fall off the Harbour Bridge while taking a selfie

2. Piss on the Opera House

3. Get pickpocketed at Paddy's Markets

4. Get melanoma at Bondi Beach

5. Spend the day sitting in a traffic jam

6. Take out a million-dollar mortgage to buy a broom cupboard in Redfern

7. Get seasick on the Manly ferry

8. Start a race riot

9. Root an entire NRL team

10. Go home at 1 a.m. when everything closes

Wollongong

Wollongong is synonymous with most words starting with 'un': uncultured, unsafe, uninspiring, unclean, unsightly, undeniably unpleasant, unemployment, unprotected sex, unconsciousness and uncle-dads. Full of decaying buildings and relying on a raft of dying heavy industries, the crime-ridden industrial wasteland is essentially a rustier version of Newcastle.

Commonly called 'The Gong' because of all the bashings, Wollongong is home to a wide swathe of undesirable characters including drunken deros, strung-out needle fiends and an inexplicable number of personal trainers. Popular activities include getting caught in a coalmine explosion, getting glassed in Crown Street Mall, getting stabbed at the railway station and getting beaten up for having the wrong colour shirt or skin. Former lord mayor Frank Arkell once coined the phrase 'Wonderful Wollongong' to promote the city—then again, former lord mayor Frank Arkell was an alleged paedophile who ended up being brutally murdered in his own home, which somewhat undermines his slogan.

Aside from general violence and disrepair, Wollongong is famous for its beaches, which is fortunate because any length of time in town will leave you with the overwhelming desire to walk into the sea. Unfortunately, said beaches are all massively polluted by both local litterbugs and Port Kembla, the city's primary cancer complex and coal export/heroin import docks. Wollongong features two

lighthouses, each as shit as the other: Wollongong Breakwater Lighthouse, which doesn't work, and Wollongong Head Lighthouse, which looks like a giant tampon.

TOWN SLOGAN Newcastle for People Who Have Given Up.

ALSO KNOWN AS The Gong, Woolly, Wollongronk, Wollonwrong, Wollonbong, Woollydong.

Nowra

There are contrasting theories as to the origin of Nowra's name. Some say it's a European butchering of the local Aboriginal word for black cockatoo. Others suggest it refers to the town being only a-Nowra-way from Wollongong. Others insist Nowra is an acronym for 'Number Of Welfare Recipients Astronomical'. One thing everyone can agree upon is that Nowra is an epically shit town.

Founded by a convict and populated by packs of deadshits and fuckwits, Nowra is basically the set of a failed Chris Lilley show. Despite being the South Coast region's commercial and administrative centre, Nowra is somehow completely devoid of jobs, leaving its residents with nothing to do but biff shopping trolleys into the river or get in a glass fight at Posties. Despite a lack of activities, the town is filled with swarms of moronic tourists from Sydney and Canberra who neglected to do any research before going on holiday.

While the South Coast has some aesthetic appeal, Nowra is a gaping hole, giving the region the nickname 'Donut'. The saltwater Shoalhaven River acts as a moat for flog-filled North Nowra and Bomaderry, shielding them from the bogan scum on the 'wrong side of the bridge'. East Nowra is the shining turd in the Nowra toilet, while Worrigee is also shit mainly because it's next to East Nowra. If you're looking for a shit suburb, you simply can't go wrong in a town whose only purpose is making Wollongong look good.

Wagga Wagga

Originally settled by illegal squatters, Wagga Wagga owes its continued existence to being a convenient piss stop on the deceptively named 'scenic route' between Sydney and Melbourne. The city's features include being built in a big hole, salty soil that won't grow a thing, a river that's filthy when it enters town and even filthier when it exits, and a silty riverbank that locals refer to as a 'beach'. Wagga Waggans are obsessed with the 'five o'clock wave', a batshit local legend that at 5 a.m. and 5 p.m. each day a giant wave flushes a secret nutrient into the Murrumbidgee River which makes all the locals good at sports. By the looks of the river, the secret nutrient is poo.

Wagga Wagga is a keen sports town, if you count stealing and burning cars as a sport. Other local interests include drunkenly downing a greasy kebab from JD's, trying to root a roomful of barely legal students at Rom's, and racism. It's appropriate that 'Wagga Wagga' sounds like Fozzie Bear's catchphrase, considering the place is full of muppets.

Desperate to shed its accurate reputation as a crime-riddled cesspit and encourage tourists to come and see its world-class array of abandoned warehouses, Wagga Wagga has co-opted the slogan 'So Nice They Named it Twice'. However, this slogan loses weight when you consider that it could equally apply to shitholes like Woy Woy, Kurri Kurri or Albury-Wodonga. A more accurate version would be 'So Much Ice They Named it Twice'.

MOST FAMOUS PERSON Dame Edna Everage, renowned as the most attractive Wagga Wagga woman of all time.

DID YOU KNOW? 'Wagga Wagga' is actually short for 'Wagga Wagga'.

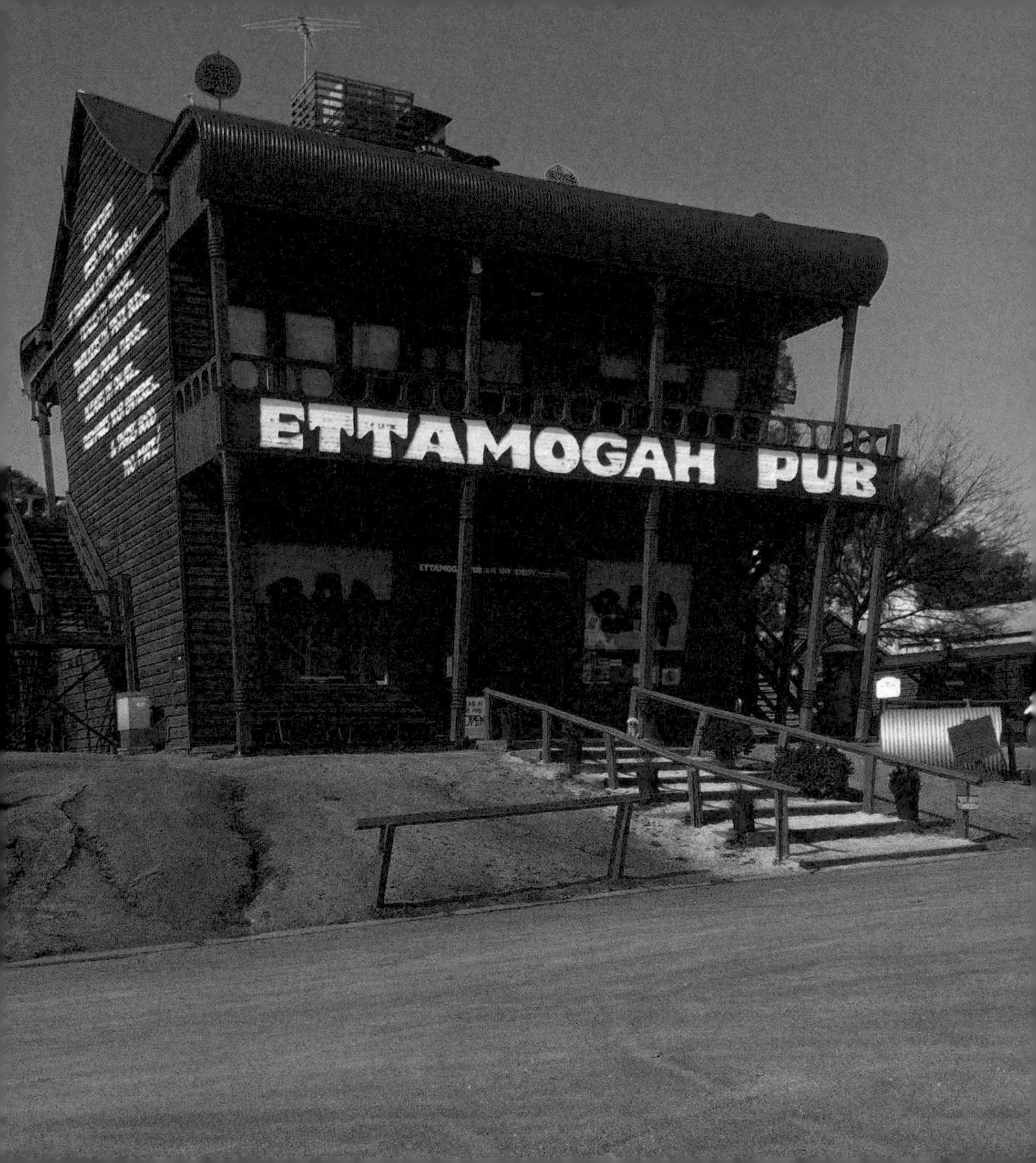
ETTAMOGAH PUB

Albury-Wodonga

Conjoined siblings straddling two states, Albury and Wodonga are twin turds in a shit sandwich. Albury on the New South Wales side is the dominant shithole, while Victoria's Wodonga is the smaller, less prosperous runt of the family. If Albury is where New South Wales dumps its undesirables, Wodonga is where Albury dumps theirs.

Together, Albury and Wodonga exist primarily as a defecation station for travellers between Sydney and Melbourne. The federal government tried to turn Albury-Wodonga into a major city in the 1970s but gave up after failing to convince anyone to move there—apparently, punters were not convinced by the blockbuster pitch of a bipolar climate, foul-smelling factories and mysterious diseases. Albury's premier landmarks are a paper mill that bathes both cities in an intolerable stench and the nearby Ettamogah Pub, an old family restaurant based on a cartoon. Wodonga's best attempt at an attraction is the world's largest rolling pin, which is about as impressive as a genital wart.

Perhaps the best sign of a truly shit town is when it has a disease named after it. Christmas Eye, also known as Albury-Wodonga syndrome, is an annual epidemic of corneal ulceration that occurs almost exclusively in and around the twin cities each summer, which may explain why everyone there looks like Forest Whitaker. Then again, it might be the meth.

NEXT
2 km

AUSTRALIAN CAPITAL TERRITORY

A bullshit pretend territory created by New South Wales as an elaborate scheme to evict Canberra, the ACT endures as a minimum-security prison for politicians, civil servants and other professional parasites. Mind-numbingly boring, bracingly ugly and boasting Australia's highest ratio of wankers per capita, the ACT is also notorious for its sub-zero winters, when it's not uncommon to find Canberra's effluent pond Lake Burley Griffin fully frozen over.

Canberra

Existing solely as a last resort capital compromise between Sydney and Melbourne, Canberra somehow manages to be Australia's smut capital and most boring city at the same time. It's known for being one of the country's only 'planned' cities, with the unfortunate consequence that its neatly ordered streets and sprawling suburbs that stretch halfway to Sydney have rendered the nation's capital an antiseptic bore with all the charm of a failed Soviet state.

The planned city received a whole slew of idiotic proposed names that somehow made 'Canberra' seem like a good option, including Home, Austral, Andy Man, Unison and Frazer Roo. One joker even proposed the horrific portmanteau Sydmeladperho, a name so massively shithouse it might have actually been able to accurately reflect Canberra's shitness. Instead, the powers-that-were plumped for Canberra, a name derived from the Aboriginal 'Nganbara' meaning 'boobs', an appropriate nod to its sleazy reputation.

Populated entirely by overpaid and underworked bureaucrats, parasitic scandal-embroiled politicians, ex-prime ministers, soon-to-be ex-prime ministers, sweaty porn barons, Chinese spies and kangaroos, Canberra is a town that celebrates flagrant corruption, rampant nepotism and beige blandness. The boring burg is renowned for revelling in the sort of culture that people only pretend to like so they can root uni students. The most prominent attractions are snooze-inducing dusty museums and stuffy art galleries, great fun for pseudo-intellectual dryballs (of which Canberra has an abundance) and punishment for everyone else. Canberra's lack of nightlife means they are only able to attract rugby league players who aren't interested in hanging out with outlaw bikie gangs or getting into public brawls, which is probably why they haven't won a comp since 1994.

There are only three reasons to visit Canberra: for a mandatory school trip, to roll the prime minister, or on a nefarious mish to Fyshwick. Originally built as a concentration camp for German prisoners in 1918, the eerily uninhabited suburb of Fyshwick is a great place to buy a used car to do a drive-by, a shipment of no-longer-legal fireworks or a bale of hardcore pornography. Fyshwick was Australia's undisputed porn mecca in the days before the internet or personal defoliation, which is why Canberra is known as the 'Bush Capital'. The sordid suburb is also home to a shopping centre called COC, appropriately located on Iron Knob Street. Fyshwick's influence is evident throughout the city: Belconnen proudly hosts an infamous penis-shaped owl sculpture, while Canberra celebrated its centenary in 2013 by commissioning a giant hot air balloon covered in tits.

TOWN SLOGAN Pyongyang in the Bush!

ALSO KNOWN AS Canbrah, Canboring, Wankberra, Cansylvania, Cuntberra.

TEN THINGS TO DO IN CANBERRA

1. Go to Sydney

2. Go to Melbourne

3. Roll the prime minister

4. Squander taxpayers' money on a series of unsound projects designed to placate voters in a marginal seat

5. Impregnate a junior staff member

6. Roll the prime minister (again)

7. Call a snap election

8. Pick up the latest copy of *Grannies Get Fanny* in Fyshwick

9. Pass legislation that allows wealthy interest groups to show blatant disregard for your constituents

10. Roll the prime minister (again)

AUSTRALIA'S WORST 'BIG THINGS'

Under Australian law, for a settlement to officially qualify as a town it must feature a giant novelty sculpture of its favourite thing alongside its nearest highway or main road, so that tourists and roadtrippers can take photos of themselves pretending to have sex with it. Consequently, Australia is awash with enormous fibreglass fruits and concrete creatures, ranging from the merely cringeworthy to the stuff of nightmares. Here are some of Australia's worst 'Big Things'.

Coffs Harbour's Big Banana

The only thing sadder than basing your entire town's tourism industry around a big phallic fruit is choosing one as generic as a banana. The Coffs monument's uniqueness and therefore reason to exist have been shattered by similar erections in Mackay, QLD and Carnarvon, WA.

Banana's Big Bull

That is not a typo. There is indeed a town in Queensland called Banana and, instead of having a big banana as you'd expect, it has a big bull. Granted, the sculpture is based on a bull called Banana who founded the town before generously inviting humans to moove in, but the lack of a big banana in Banana is an egregious violation of all logic and, quite frankly, un-Australian. Unsurprisingly, we have serious beef with this bull.

Berri's Big Orange

Just like Banana opting for a big bull rather than the thing in its name, the South Australian town of Berri has infuriatingly plumped for a gigantic orange. We hereby challenge the Berri brains trust to either gift the Big Orange to Orange in New South Wales or slap it with a red coat of paint and call it a 'cranberri'.

Ballina's Big Prawn

There's a reason prawns are small: so we don't have to be confronted by their creepy crustacean features at full size—until now. Plonked in the car park of Ballina Bunnings, the Big Prawn is enough to put any home handyman off their Sunday sausage sizzle.

Goulburn's Big Merino

Whoever designed this fifteen-metre-tall monstrosity was obviously given a brief to make it look as hideous as humanly possible. Covered from head to foot in flabby folds, the Big Merino looks more like a tumour than a sheep. Adding to its indignity is a set of giant testicles on full display. The Big Merino has also been ripped off by Wagin in Western Australia, which has its own similarly ugly version complete with massive scrotum. For more big animal balls, seek out Rockhampton's disturbingly anatomically accurate Big Bulls.

Rockhampton's Big Dugong

As if its seven Big Bulls weren't enough, Rockhampton decided to add a massive statue of the world's ugliest marine mammal to the mix. Flopped lazily on the floor doing fuck-all, the flabby beast is an appropriate representation of the Beef Capital's inhabitants.

Augathella's Big Meat Ant

Unlike Broken Hill's Big Ant, this thing actually looks like one, which makes it a truly terrifying spectacle. Local authorities in the remote Queensland town are reportedly at a loss as to why the Big Meat Ant has failed to attract the waves of tourists they had anticipated.

Humpty Doo's Big Boxing Crocodile

Frozen in an unnatural pose in a shithole town just outside Darwin, this massive boxing croc, complete with shiny red gloves, is one of Australia's strangest Big Things, not to mention the most unrealistic.

Taree's Big Oyster

Originally an unsuccessful restaurant and souvenir shop, the Big Oyster's popularity has not increased since it became a car dealership. With a mouthful of windows that look disturbingly like teeth, it's no wonder this yonic yawner is known locally as the 'Big Mistake'.

Kew's Big Axe

Hanging menacingly over the tiny townsfolk below, blade pointing downwards, this eight-metre-tall weapon is Australia's most sinister Big Thing.

Kalgoorlie's Big Bin

Fittingly for a dumpster fire of a town, Kalgoorlie's attempt at a Big Thing is a giant rubbish bin—or to be accurate, an eight-metre length of rusty pipe with some handles and 'World's Tallest Bin' painted on it. The Big Bin was installed as a promotional prop to discourage littering, despite the irony that it is far too tall for anyone to use.

Larrimah's Big Stubby

As if a classic NT Draught 'Darwin Stubby' weren't already big enough, an even bigger version exists in Larrimah. Sitting outside a pub in the middle of Northern Territory nowhere, the only way the Big Stubby could be a greater celebration of good old-fashioned Aussie alcoholism is if it were a big goon box.

Mourquong's Big Goon Box

Celebrating the aero's drop of choice, a winery near the tiny Mildura satellite of Mourquong transformed a shed into a giant box of the old Chateau Cardboard. The Big Wine Cask has since been painted over, to the great disappointment of the region's myriad bogans.

Maitland's Big Ugg Boots

Speaking of bogans, everyone's favourite trashy footwear is glorified by the Big Ugg Boots, which sit outside the Mortels Sheepskin Factory in Thornton, Maitland.

Woodenbong's Big Wooden Bong

Standing a massive ten metres tall and carved from a solid tree trunk, Woodenbong's Big Wooden Bong has been a family photo favourite for generations, and would be impressive except for the fact that an actual wooden bong would be entirely impractical due to water rot. The only solution is to change the town's name to Glassbong or Gatoradebottlebong and redo it.

Nyngan's Big Bogan

Just when you thought things couldn't possibly get any more bogan than a goon box and a bong, Nyngan has abandoned all subtlety and erected a Big Bogan. The two-dimensional mulleted, goateed, patriotic-tattoo-adorned, wife-beater-wearing, esky-toting bloke celebrates the town's status as the main centre of the unfortunately named Bogan Shire. Not depicted are the Big Bogan's Big Holden Commodore with its Big Racist Bumper Sticker.

Cairns's Big Nazi

Cairns's towering statue of Captain Cook giving an unmistakable Hitler salute might just be the worst Big Thing of all time. Could it be the work of a secret Nazi sympathiser, or perhaps a sneaky comment on colonisation? More likely it's just another poorly designed, poorly executed Big Thing.

Byron Bay's Big Dildo

The tourist hotspot of Byron Bay has the dubious honour of being the only town in Australia to rock an oversized replica sex toy, with its infamous giant disco dong. The massive silver phallus sits on a roundabout at the entrance to town, making it the first thing visitors see upon arrival.

Robertson's Big Potato

The main tourist attraction of Robertson, New South Wales barely qualifies as a Big Thing as it's basically just a septic tank that someone painted brown and called a potato. Obviously designed by someone who had never seen a spud before, it looks more like a poo than a potato.

Kiama's Big Poo

Speaking of faeces, Big Things don't get any more shit than Kiama's Big Poo. Commissioned by a New South Wales MP, the five-metre-long foam turd sits right next to the 'Welcome to Kiama' sign on the Princes Highway, warning all travellers of Kiama's shit town status.

VICTORIA

Home of the AFL—the world's most elaborate homosexual mating ritual—and filled with more moustachioed hipsters than a ukulele concert, Victoria is Australia's capital of smug self-righteousness and faux-European sophistication. As the smallest mainland state and having been overlooked as the location of the nation's capital, Victoria is also famous for the chip on its collective shoulder. Victorians are commonly referred to as Cabbage Patchers, Gum Suckers or Mexicans.

Mildura

Sitting on the shores of the muddy, toxic, algae-filled Murray River and tucked just inside the Victorian border, Mildura owes its existence to an irrigation experiment that transformed it from an arid wasteland into a soggy wasteland that grows fruit. The city's horticultural heritage is reflected in the names of its streets, including Orange Avenue, Lemon Avenue and Avocado Street. In recent times more modern industries have also been honoured in similar fashion: Chroming Street, Insurance Fraud Avenue and Handjob Boulevard.

Mildura calls itself 'Victoria's Food Bowl', but 'Meth Bowl' would be more accurate. The original translation of Mildura is 'sore eyes', which is strangely appropriate considering the average Milduran's scabby peepers have been prised open on a six-week drug binge. Aside from picking fruit for slave wages, popular activities in 'Methdura' include living in a van down by the river, staying awake for three weeks in a row and trading sexual favours for a suck on the see-through didgeridoo.

Mildura is the capital of 'Sunraysia', a made-up country populated by sun-worshipping gronks. It's also the welfare fraud capital of Victoria, proving that Mildurans enjoy a spot of dole bludging as much as they like actively courting melanoma. Another local obsession involves relentlessly revving anything with an engine, whether a powerboat on the river or a rusted boganmobile with a baked beans tin for an exhaust—anything incredibly loud and obnoxious will do when you're poorly endowed and want the whole world to know.

TOWN SLOGAN	Melons, Meth and Microdicks.
ALSO KNOWN AS	Mildewra, Methdura.

FAN MAIL

Shepparton is NOT a shit town mate; You are! **(JULIUS SMUDGE, SHEPPARTON)**

You're a fucken cockhead you brain dead piece of shit. **(JOSE MARZIPAN JNR, BENDIGO)**

How about you shove your shit towns of Australia up your arse! **(DOUGLAS WHEELBARROW, BALLARAT)**

Get a life you peanuts. **(BERTHA LACERATION, MELBOURNE)**

FUCK OF you fuck Tart **(ROSSO MARCELI, CANBERRA)**

Shepparton

Originally named McGuire's Punt by some bloke with a dirty mind and poor spelling skills, Shepparton began life as a sheep station before transforming into a bustling rail hub and finally ending up in its current incarnation as a smouldering post-apocalyptic crater. The name Shepparton is a portmanteau of the city's two favourite things: sheep and methamphetamine. Shepparton's tourism slogan is 'Many Great Things', which is at best a charitable exaggeration and at worst blatant false advertising. What Shepparton lacks in culture, entertainment, nightlife and water it makes up for in drugs, bogans, teenage pregnancy and the ubiquitous scent of cow shit.

Common hobbies in Shepparton include jamming fruit into tins, doing lappies along Wyndham Street in your souped-up debtmobile and having your welfare payments quarantined. Maude Street Mall is a popular spot for drug deals and knife fights, while the ironically named Olympic Avenue wins the gold medal for 'getting stabbed with a broken VB stubby'. The largest, nicest and busiest building in Shepparton is the courthouse.

Shepparton displays a collection of life-size fibreglass cows in public spaces as a tribute to the life-size actual cows that used to roam the town before an enterprising Sheppartard swapped them all for a clapped-out Commodore. The Shepparton Art Museum houses the world's most significant collection of Australian ceramics, which is also the world's most boring thing to collect. The main event in

Shepparton is the Spring Car Nationals, a giant magnet for wild packs of criminals and fume-huffing hoons and a particularly great time not to visit.

TOWN SLOGAN Shepprazent!

ALSO KNOWN AS Shep, Shepp, Sheppo, Shittarton, Methamphetarton, Sheppatitis.

Bendigo

Originally a squalid tent city for grog-soaked gold miners, Bendigo continues to emit a feral vibe. The tents are now housing commission slums, the diggers are now bogans and the alcoholism is now alcoholism. Still sporting the carcasses of long-abandoned mines, Bendigo is like a Scooby Doo ghost town, but instead of elderly caretakers creating phantoms with torches and combs, it's full of meatheads cracking stubbies with their eye sockets.

Popular activities in 'Bendighetto' include being chased by bats, being chased by bogans with bats, chasing bogans with bats, and meth. The highlight of Bendigo's social calendar is the annual car parts swap meet each November, when Bendigonads buy back all the bits they had stolen throughout the year. For people masochistic enough to visit Bendigo, attractions include an array of musty mining museums, crusty old heritage buildings and dusty potteries.

A popular piece of trivia is that Bendigo was named after a boxer, foreshadowing the city's beloved tradition of bare-knuckle fighting. Less commonly known is that it also shares its name with a rare syndrome which causes extreme curvature of the penis. The syndrome is most likely to affect men who wear budgie smugglers for prolonged periods, such as lifeguards, competitive swimmers and Tony Abbott.

Wherever you go, don't go to Bendigo.

ALSO KNOWN AS Bendy, Benders, Bongdigo, Bendighetto, Bendiblow, Bendigonad.

ICONIC LANDMARK Bendigo boasts a selection of baffling sculptures, including one of a man being mercilessly mauled by a lion and a wolf.

DID YOU KNOW? Bendigo earned international fame when its extreme bogan-ness earned it a cameo in the animated documentary series *Rick and Morty*.

Ballarat

Founded during the gold rush, Ballarat began life as a ramshackle shanty town populated by thousands of grubby diggers. Around 150 years later it has completely transformed into a ramshackle city populated by thousands of grubby housos.

In its early days, Ballarat earned the moniker 'the Golden City' due to locals' fondness for golden showers, while residents also referred to it as 'the Athens of Australia' due to their predilection for anal sex. The deviance continues to this day with the city lending its name to the 'Ballarat cravat', a euphemism for the popular Ballarat activity of shotgunning a blast of diarrhoea all over another person's neck.

Ballarat is perhaps best known for the Eureka Rebellion, when a bunch of gold-grabbers took up arms against the government because they couldn't be fucked paying tax. Ironically, these violent immigrants who refused to assimilate are now lauded as heroes by rednecks across the country, with the Eureka flag enduring as Australia's second-favourite white supremacist icon after the Southern Cross tattoo.

Ballarat's proudest feature is Lake Wendouree which half the time has no water in it, making it more of a hole than a lake. Wendouree was originally called Black Swamp before being renamed after an Aboriginal word meaning 'go away'.

When it's not baking hot enough to evaporate a lake, Ballarat defaults to freezing cold. It's also known for its poor air quality, being

smoky as a bogan's breath in winter and dustier than your mum's muff in summer, ensuring it is a truly terrible place to visit at any time of year.

TOWN SLOGAN Once a Slum, Always a Slum.

ALSO KNOWN AS B-Rat, Rat City, The Rat, Hellarat, Smellarat, Ballacrap, Ball-a-Rat.

Melbourne

Melbourne has long been considered Australia's bohemian capital, a bulging flogatropolis full of hirsute hipsters, craft beer wankers, militant vegans and 'entrepreneurs' blagging on about cryptocurrencies and angel investors. Melburnians' favourite hobbies include moaning about Sydney, munching organic quinoa served on a garbage bin lid, pretending to understand foreign films, blockading streets because hamburgers made them sad, using heroin, and making dirty alleys sound quaint by calling them 'laneways'.

Victoria's capital also claims to be the country's sport capital, as locals are all either obsessed with sport to a sexual degree or make a point of hating sport in order to appear different. The city is the epicentre of the national AFL epidemic, a game so retarded it could only have been conceived by a convict with heatstroke and too much time on his hands. For those unacquainted with this rather esoteric sport, a 'Sherrin' is the ball, a 'sausage roll' is a goal and 'the Brownlow' is something that you might get after the grand final if your missus has had enough shiraz.

Melbourne was founded after a joker called John Batman swindled the land from its Indigenous residents and christened it Batmania. Today the city features a Batman Avenue and a Batman Park, which would be awesome if they weren't named after a syphilitic mass murderer. For much of Melbourne's history since, the city has been held by the gonads by organised crime groups that run massive drug, racketeering and assassination operations, but thanks to politicians and the media, locals are more afraid of fictional 'African gangs' tagging their fence.

ALSO KNOWN AS Melbs, Batmania, Melbyville, Melboring, Smellbourne.

MOST FAMOUS PERSON Mark 'Chopper' Read, a serial killer turned terrible rapper and children's author who had his own ears cut off and smeared faeces in his enemies' faces, making him almost as mental as your average Collingwood supporter.

TEN THINGS TO DO IN MELBOURNE

1. Buy an overpriced coffee from a moustachioed wanker who looks like an Edwardian pimp

2. Get run over by a tram

3. Take a shit in a laneway

4. Witness the Victorian homoerotic ritual called 'the AFL'

5. Immerse yourself in Melbourne's 'street art' culture by spray painting your name on some bastard's wall

6. Join the political racial panic over 'African gangs'

7. Enjoy a local 'craft beer', i.e. normal beer with kerosene and cum in it

8. Die in a gangland shooting

9. Grow a man bun to hide your crippling lack of self-esteem

10. Get stabbed by a Collingwood fan

Geelong

Geelong is renowned for having more terrible nicknames than any other city in Australia, including 'The Pivot', 'Sleepy Hollow', 'Gateway City' (due to its proliferation of gateway drugs), 'The Small Smoke', 'Geetroit' and 'Shit Melbourne'. It's also known as Victoria's 'Number Two City' because it's the state's second-largest, it's home to the second-oldest Aussie Rules football club, and it's a big pile of shit. The phrase 'second place is the first loser' was invented for Geelong.

Geelong is home to a staggering array of bogans, hicks and rednecks. It has a lively nightlife scene, if by 'nightlife' you mean 'packs of pissed-up drongos rampaging down Moorabool Street'. The suburbs of Corio and Norlane are two of the world's largest open-air bogan sanctuaries, where visitors can watch yobbos get a Southern Cross tattoo, shoplift a case of VB and spend their Centrelink on meth in their natural habitat. Geelong also features an impressive collection of lead-contaminated water fountains—the city is so bogan that even its bubblers are filled with heavy metal.

Geelong's status as a cultural wasteland is highlighted by its best attempts at visitor attractions: a wool museum, an abandoned car factory, and an army of truly nightmarish bollard people. The city's favourite sports team is the Geelong Cats, an AFL club that borrowed its nickname, team song and playing squad from a girls' under-nines netball team.

TASMANIA

Filled with feral clans of two-headed Tasmaniacs and subsisting on a variety of primary industries that died in the late twentieth century, Tasmania is a hotbed of incest and cannibalism. The island state's mascot is the Tasmanian devil, a vicious dog-sized rat with a demonic screech and disgusting facial disease. Tasmania also used to be famous for the thylacine, or Tasmanian tiger, but the state government paid people to kill them until they went extinct. Fun fact: 'Map of Tassie' is slang for a woman's pubic region.

TEN THINGS TO DO IN TASMANIA

1. Become the subject of a podcast about mysterious disappearances

2. Contract a rare strain of gonorrhoea

3. Try a locally made human steak

4. Introduce the locals to the modern wonders of cell phones, the internet and soap

5. Become a locally made human steak

6. Burn off your hand by touching the Derwent River

7. Become strangely aroused by a blood relative

8. Start a website warning the public about the dangers of chemtrails

9. Marry your hot sister

10. Escape to the mainland

Launceston

It's well established that large numbers of Tasmanians are descended from the worst convicts exiled to Australia, so they have a frightening tendency towards cannibalism, incest and being Ricky Ponting. Nowhere are these three crimes against humanity better exemplified than the island state's secondary city, Launceston.

Launceston is best known as the home town of two of Australia's most celebrated cricketers: the aforementioned Ponting, a.k.a. Mr Magoo with 1970s Lego-man hair, and human fire hydrant David Boon. Both have represented their town impeccably on the world stage, Boon by once smashing 52 tins on a flight from Sydney to London—a feat which saw him awarded the coveted Australian of the Year Award—and Ponting by being one quarter wombat and famously getting beaten up by a transvestite.

Launceston is home to the world's longest single span chairlift, which was originally constructed as an escape route from frequent flooding. It was also the site of the first use of anaesthetic in the Southern Hemisphere, which was developed to numb the pain of living in Launceston. The city's premier attraction is a colony of herpes B–riddled Japanese macaque monkeys that bizarrely live in an enclosure in City Park, making it one of the world's best places to catch a potentially fatal STI from a monkey. Another tourist drawcard is the Old Umbrella Shop, a rare example of an intact early twentieth-century store, complete with golliwogs in the window. Other than buying racist toys, popular pastimes in Launceston include trying to figure out how to pronounce the city's name and playing a stupid sport called vigoro, the inbred bastard child of cricket and tennis.

There's no shame in coming second, unless it's coming second to Hobart.

TOWN SLOGAN Tasmania's Number Two!

ALSO KNOWN AS Lonny, Lunny, Lawny, Inceston.

FAN MAIL

You have a real problem a selfish naracustic
person. **(NELSON FUNGUS, LAUNCESTON)**

What a twolt that wrote this. And learn to spell. Queentown,
Where was you educated? **(MARTY GLAND, QUEENSTOWN)**

Written by someone that perfumes there
own arse. **(QUINCY LESTRANGE, HOBART)**

Queenstown

Buried deep in Tasmania's terrifying western wastelands, the nightmarish hellhole of Queenstown could not be more incongruous with its regal moniker. The living museum of misery comprises a cluster of dilapidated hovels and abandoned shacks with mangy dogs chained up outside, perching on the precipice of an abandoned copper mine, surrounded by slag heaps and adorned with a polluted, poo-filled river. Despite being subject to incessant rain, Queenstown's tap water is brown and undrinkable. Decades of deforestation, sulphurous smelter fumes and topsoil erosion have rendered the area's hills a barren moonscape. Famously featuring a gravel footy oval because grass refuses to grow there, Queenstown is a great place to visit if you get your rocks off on mass-scale ecological vandalism. Locals are so proud of their desolate wasteland that they have opposed revegetation attempts. Queenstown is not so much a town as an inhabited environmental disaster.

Despite being a half-abandoned soggy little slum, Queenstown's understandably cheap housing attracts undesirables from all over Australia, including extreme hermits who can't handle the hustle and bustle of Hobart and extreme hillbillies who require extra privacy for nefarious habits like marrying their siblings or eating tourists. The town's defunct mining business has been replaced by a fledgling tourism industry, predicated entirely on befuddled travellers ending up there by accident after trying to reach its New Zealand namesake.

The dismal little village was strategically built in a hole among the mountains to hinder escape—visitors are forced to negotiate a rollercoaster road with over 90 hair-raising bends just to get out of the place.

A third-world shithole as quaint as a yeast infection, Queenstown is a foolproof recipe for getting instant depression.

TOWN SLOGAN Cloudy With a Chance of Acid Rain.

ALSO KNOWN AS Queeftown, Rainy Mordor.

Hobart

Founded as a human shit pit for Britain's surplus riffraff, Hobart soon grew into a town after becoming a major centre for the murder of endangered sea creatures. Today, Tasmania's capital is populated by 200,000 seal clubbers, 'chiggers' (bogans, but more inbred) and pseudo-hipsters who think they're cosmopolitan because they live in their island's biggest city even though they have never left Tasmania. The main industries in Hobart are freeloading off the mainland, poisoning the water with zinc, clear-felling primeval rainforests, whingeing about mainlanders, and crying about not having an AFL team.

Hobart's proudest feature is its historic buildings, built using convict slave labour. The main tourist attraction is the Museum of Old and New Art, which is lucky because most Tasmanians can't read. Another feature is the ruins of the Hobart Zoo, complete with suicidal-looking cartoon animals adorning its dilapidated gate. For unknown reasons, fleets of norovirus-afflicted cruise ships choose to dock in Hobart for the saddest stop of their journey.

Hobart is a 'fusion city', in that it marries big city problems with small town facilities. Despite being completely shit, it's the only place in Tasmania with any jobs and has thus been inundated by hordes of Tasmaniacs, causing a rental crisis that has forced despos to live in tents at the showgrounds. 'Slowbart' also has a horrendous traffic problem, with no public transport beyond buses and somehow more cars than people. The turd-filled Derwent River is massively polluted by heavy metals from the zinc works, meaning it's unsafe to eat certain fish. Zinc leaching has also contaminated the groundwater, making homegrown vegetables poisonous in some suburbs, disproving the claim by millions of mums that broccoli can't hurt you. Clearly, the only good thing to do in the toxic joint is leave.

ALSO KNOWN AS Hobarton, Hofart, Hobarf, Ho Town.

MOST FAMOUS PERSON Famous Hobartians include actor and accused rapist Errol Flynn and notorious cannibal Alexander Pearce.

SOUTH AUSTRALIA

The only state not colonised by convicts, South Australia has attempted to make up for it ever since by churning out more serial killers, paedophiles and cannibals than any other state. Not content with being filled with more murderers than a Milat family reunion, South Australia also does a nice line in stultifying boredom. If being bored to death or hacked to pieces in gruesome fashion aren't your idea of a good time, be sure to give the state of the 'Croweaters' a wide berth.

Mount Gambier

Mount Gambier is best known for its pillars of limestone and mountains of meth. It's South Australia's ice capital, and not just because its winter is cold enough to freeze off your dangly bits. The city's most notorious neighbourhood is the 'Crack Sac', a cluster of housing commission cul-de-sacs known as a residential mecca for illicit substances—the Westfield Marion of drugs.

As well as housing enough ice to sink the *Titanic*, Mount Gambier is also South Australia's boredom capital, with the most popular pastime being laboriously doing mainies while waiting for the mountain to explode again and drown the town in lava and ash like some kind of bogan Pompeii. The surrounding area is pockmarked by a plague of caves, sinkholes and other abysses for unfortunate tourists to stare into and contemplate the meaninglessness of existence and the folly of their decision to visit. One of the largest sinkholes is Hells Hole, not to be confused with the town of Mount Gambier, which is a hellhole. The second biggest hole in the area—after the town—is the Blue Lake, which was discovered and named by early explorer Captain James Obvious. Despite its name, the Blue Lake is only blue in summer; at other times it is known as Murky Grey Lake.

Mount Gambier promotes itself with the slogan 'City Meets Country', which means it has both ice and incest. Another popular slogan is 'Mount Gambier: Gateway to the Limestone Coast and Meth Addiction'.

Adelaide

'This is Port Adelaide! Port Misery would be a better name, for nothing in any other part of the world can surpass it in everything that is wretched and inconvenient.'—THOMAS HORTON JAMES, AUTHOR

Adelaide is known as the 'City of Churches, Pubs and Serial Killers'. The city's roll of gory crimes includes a series of gruesome murders committed by a shadowy cabal of paedophiles, a series of gruesome murders committed by a bunch of drongos on the dole, and Jimmy Barnes's musical career. Despite its delusions of cityhood, South Australia's capital is essentially an overgrown country town complete with high unemployment, shit public transport, shops only opening for a few hours per weekday, undrinkable drinking water, rampant racism and an almost Tasmanian level of cousin-fucking. Adelaide is populated by an array of junkies, thugs and gronks, as any Adelaideans resembling normal humans waste no time in moving to Melbourne or Sydney.

Adelaide is a favourite spot for the federal government to house its expensive fuck-ups, including a submarine fleet that had difficulty submerging and an expensive desalination plant that does fuck-all. The city's most cherished invention is the Hills hoist, which is a type of clothesline that was originally dreamed up as a mechanism for tanning the hides of flayed hitchhikers. Farmers Union Iced Coffee is considered a local delicacy and has been known to outsell Coca-Cola in Adelaide, despite the fact that it tastes like an ashtray full of Nescafe.

Adelaide Zoo is proudly home to Australia's only pandas. This pride is somewhat mitigated by the fact that in true South Australian fashion the pandas refuse to mate, dedicating their days to the standard Adelaide pursuits of getting on the goon and going late-night shopping at Westfield Marion. Another hot shopping spot is Rundle Mall, a classy establishment adorned with statues of pigs rummaging through bins and a pair of giant gonads known as 'the Mall's Balls'.

Very few tourists ever visit Adelaide intentionally, with the largest number of visitors citing 'got shitfaced on a stag and my mates thought it would be funny to put me on a plane' as their reason for travelling.

ALSO KNOWN AS Radelaide, Sadelaide, Badelaide, Marmalade, Bladderlaide, Port Misery.

MOST FAMOUS PERSON 'Cocaine' Cassie Sainsbury, Adelaide's own shit Schapelle Corby.

TEN THINGS TO DO IN ADELAIDE

1. Get abused by a racist old person

2. Get abused by a racist bogan

3. Get abused by a racist junkie

4. Get abused by a racist paedophile

5. Get rinsed on an overpriced chardonnay

6. Build a fleet of defective submarines

7. Get diarrhoea after eating a pie floater

8. Fondle the Mall's Balls

9. Catch salmonella from an iced coffee

10. Hide some decomposing bodies in an abandoned bank vault

Port Pirie

Sitting (and shitting) on a polluted tidal river replete with lead-poisoned dolphins, the seaside smelter town of Port Pirie possesses all the charm of a soiled man-nappy. Port Pirie is home to the world's largest lead smelter, an operation so significant that its stack is the highest structure in the state, billowing clouds of toxic fumes like a bogan Eye of Sauron. The smelter employs 10 per cent of the town's population, making lead manufacturing the second most common job in Port Pirie after 'unemployed' at 11 per cent. Another 4 per cent work in animal husbandry, which in South Australia is exactly what it sounds like.

Aside from producing copious amounts of heavy metals, Port Pirie's smelter also poisons the town's sea, air and drinking water, resulting in a population of brain-dead lead-heads. This is one possible explanation for the Bridge to Nowhere, a road bridge that leads to a completely empty patch of land for no apparent reason. It also possibly explains Port Pirie's problem with antisocial behaviour, from the elevated levels of racism and country music to the large lady who famously flashed her K-cups at the Google Street View car. Low-lying Port Pirie proves that you don't need hills to have hillbillies.

TOWN SLOGANS The Chernobyl of the South; Mount Isa by the Sea.

ALSO KNOWN AS PP, Poor Pirie, Port Shitty.

FAN MAIL

Do some research chernobyl was nuclear we are lead get of ya sister and find a real life drop kick. **(GUS MINTO, PORT PIRIE)**

WHAT A LOAD OF SHIT 15 YEARS AGO THEY HAD THE MOST PEOPLE LIVING OVER 90 PER CAPITOR DISGUSTING COMMENTS FROM THIS INDIVIDUAL. **(TIMMY TRONC, PORT PIRIE)**

How dare you piece of shit it's not the town that's shit if you don't ever touch PT PIRIE again god bless. **(STEVE SILVA, PORT PIRIE)**

Port Augusta

Port Augusta is known as a working-class town, which is ironic because no one there has a job. The city has been redundant since its port ceased to operate in 1973, making half of its name a lie. Attempts to resuscitate 'Portagutter' by kickstarting a new economy predicated on polluting the atmosphere with copious amounts of carbon ended with the closure of all of its coal-fired power plants in the last decade. Now little more than a blight on the South Australian desert landscape, Port Augusta exists purely so people can confuse it with Port Pirie and Port Lincoln.

Port Augusta's most famous feature is its putrid stench, courtesy of a dried-up tyre-filled mud puddle called Bird Lake, which makes the entire city smell almost as bad as its residents. The place is cursed with a punishing climate that sees the mercury push 50 degrees, forcing feral locals to cool off in the flooded rubbish tip known as the Spencer Gulf. Five hundred algae-encrusted shopping trolleys were recently fished up from waters near the wharf to prevent jumpers from landing on them, but a sizeable trolley reef remains.

Aside from a derelict disused port, Port Disgusta boasts a world-class collection of abandoned buildings, towering razor-wire-tipped fences, beaches with more broken glass than sand, and patches of dirt in lieu of lawns. It's also home to the Australian Arid Lands Botanic Garden, which showcases all of the nothing that grows in the outback. A former hit with overseas visitors was the now-closed Baxter

Detention Centre, which attracted tourists from all over Southeast Asia and the Middle East and must have been incredible because most visitors stayed for years.

TOWN SLOGAN Where the Dirt Meets the Sea.

ALSO KNOWN AS Portagutter, Port Disgusta.

Coober Pedy

Coober Pedy was named from the Aboriginal 'Kupa-Piti' meaning 'white man's hole', which couldn't be more appropriate. It's also appropriate that the anglicised name evokes South Australia's unfortunate predilection for paedophilia, but Coober Pedy is a town fond of a different kind of miner as the self-proclaimed opal mining capital of the world. Consequently, the town is populated entirely by toothless, leathery opal noodlers. Popular pastimes include pillaging the earth of its precious minerals, looking at a spaceship from a Vin Diesel movie that sits on a patch of dirt next to a public toilet, and dying of heatstroke.

Situated in the middle of the South Australian outback, Coober Pedy is a post-apocalyptic hellscape so inhospitable to human life that its only inhabitants huddle in subterranean shelters like the survivors of a thermonuclear conflagration. Above ground it's a ghost town, a dusty dystopian wasteland littered with bits of rusted metal, used syringes, tumbleweed, and flea-bitten feral dogs baking in the sun while they wait for death. The only greenery in Coober Pedy is in plastic bags hidden under mattresses in its denizens' prison-like bunkers, and the only tree to be seen is a lifeless scrap iron sculpture that looms ominously over the town. Fittingly, this distinctive landscape has featured in a slew of motion pictures, from *Mad Max Beyond Thunderdome* to *Priscilla, Queen of the Desert* to the aptly named *Until the End of the World*. If someone wanted a glimpse into

Australia's future after it has been rendered an uninhabitable husk by the ravages of global warming then they could do a lot worse than visiting Coober Pedy.

ALSO KNOWN AS Goober Pedy, Coober Pedo, Poober Pedy.

NORTHERN TERRITORY

A post-apocalyptic shitscape filled with serial killers, dingo rapists and dispossessed Indigenous people, the Northern Territory is plagued by problems far too intense to probe deeply in a guidebook of this type, from the sort of poverty that most Australians refuse to believe exists to functional apartheid to whatever is up with Tennant Creek. Among the carnage is an iceberg of shit towns, the tip of which is touched on in this section.

TEN THINGS TO DO IN THE NORTHERN TERITORY

1. Die from heat exhaustion

2. Die from drinking petrol

3. Die from getting bottled with a Darwin Stubby

4. Die from getting mauled by a crocodile

5. Die from getting mauled by a shark

6. Die from getting stung by a box jellyfish

7. Die from getting eaten by a dingo

8. Die from getting eaten by a snake

9. Die from getting bitten by a venomous spider

10. Die from being murdered while backpacking in the outback

SHARK
SIGHTED
TODAY

ENTER WATER
AT OWN
RISK

Alice Springs

Australia's geographic anus, Alice Springs is an enclave of chaos in the middle of the outback. Despite having a name more suited to a menopausal jazzercise instructor, Alice Springs is known as the stabbing capital of the world, as well as one of the country's capitals of youth crime and racism.

Fittingly for Australia's arsehole, Alice Springs is full of dicks: marauding gangs of children biffing rocks at ambulances, jaundiced junkies swigging petrol straight from the bowser and rampaging rednecks beating up Aboriginal youths. It's also home to hordes of lesbians left over from 1980s feminist marches, stampeding caravans of rabid camels, packs of baby-eating dingoes and pockets of terrified tourists.

Despite a complete absence of attractions in the town itself, Alice Springs has sprung up a tourism industry as a result of its relative proximity to Uluru (or 'Ayers Rock' in Racist Old White Person). The local economy is especially reliant on international visitors as they tend to have more valuable things to steal. Unfortunately for Alice Springs, the town is so shit that the governments of several countries have advised their citizens not to go there. In fact, the only overseas town willing to become an official sister city of Alice Springs was a village in Afghanistan. Even its biological sister cities of Palm Springs and Colorado Springs refuse to publicly associate themselves with their embarrassing sibling.

Katherine

Katherine—the 'Top End' town, not that boring woman from HR—spruiks itself as 'where the outback meets the tropics', or in other words, 'where the drought meets the floods'. The town's two seasons are searing heat season, when most organic matter withers to a crisp, and thunderstorm season, when the town fills to the gills with poo-brown water and crocodiles chase kayakers through the streets.

Katherine is basically a tarted-up gulag masquerading as civilisation—Tennant Creek in drag—if you can consider fortified servos, police guards outside grog shops and a poisoned water supply an improvement. Popular pastimes in Katherine include rooting on the grass median strip on the Stuart Highway or taking a dump on the footpath outside Red Rooster. Dole day sees the entire citizenry get shitfaced and fight each other, while primary school kids riddled with preventable diseases roam the streets at all hours honing their vandalism skills. The local soundtrack is feral fruit bats screaming all day and mangy stray dogs howling all night.

Lacking any significant industry, Katherine scrapes by on tourism thanks to Katherine Gorge. The dry season sees an influx of soon-to-be-missing European backpackers as well as 'grey nomads', grizzled geriatrics escaping the southern winter so they can sit in front of their caravans and whinge about the heat. The area's biggest attraction is Nitmiluk National Park, where visitors can get up close to Katherine's big hole and some of Katherine's bush.

FAN MAIL

To the fuck-stick that posted this shit...go impale
yrself on a Darwin stubbie...you piece of Turkey shit...
you cock stretching wanker...go stick your head in
a bucket of shit!!! **(BARRY BAWDEN, ALICE SPRINGS)**

You must have gone through Katherine with your head
up your arse. I bet your not even a true Australian.
Get a real job you wanker. **(TODD MINGE, KATHERINE)**

You insult our town expect to be branded a
cockwooble **(REGINALD TRAPEZOID, DARWIN)**

Darwin

Darwin is the only city in the world with more crocodiles than human beings. It's also the only major Australian city to be levelled by the Japanese during World War II and completely destroyed by cyclones on three separate occasions, from which it has never fully recovered. The federal government maintains Darwin as a live-action replica of what could be expected to happen to a major Australian city in a nuclear apocalypse.

Popular hobbies in the Northern Territory's ramshackle capital include alcoholism, arguing over who would win a fight between a saltie and a great white, and pointing out the inaccuracies in *Wolf Creek*. The city's premier events are the annual Beer Can Regatta, in which contestants race boats made entirely out of empty booze tins while emptying several more, and NT Cracker Day, when resident youth take time out from holding up servos with kitchen knives to engage in a spot of casual arson and drive-by firework shooting.

The local agenda-setter is the *NT News*, a bastion of quality journalism responsible for such headlines as 'Horny ghost haunts house', 'Sexy granny drought' and 'Why I stuck a cracker up my clacker'.

Darwin markets itself as the 'Gateway to the Outback', despite the fact that the same slogan is claimed by every desert shithole in Australia. Darwin is also the 'Gateway to Asia', a much stronger selling point as the idea of fleeing to another continent is particularly appealing when you're in Darwin. In fact, Darwin's most popular slogan is 'Gateway to Anywhere That Isn't Fucking Darwin'.

MOST FAMOUS PERSON Bradley John Murdoch, current world champion of competitive 'hiding a body in the outback'.

WESTERN AUSTRALIA

Known as the 'Wild West' due to copious amounts of crime and general carnage, Western Australia is convinced that the rest of the country is indifferent to them, a fact confirmed by the fact that the rest of Australia routinely forgets it exists. The inhabitants of Western Australia call themselves 'sandgropers', which surprisingly doesn't refer to some desert-based Rolf Harris antics but rather a hideous burrowing insect. Western Australia overwhelmingly voted to secede from Australia in 1933 but the House of Commons refused the request, mainly to annoy them.

TEN THINGS TO DO IN WESTERN AUSTRALIA

1. Be overpaid to dig holes in the ground

2. Take a haul truck for a joy ride while high on meth

3. Get red dirt in every orifice

4. Jizz in your high-vis overalls at a skimpies night

5. Jizz in your high-vis overalls at a himpies night

6. Visit Australia's oldest brothel

7. Visit Australia's oldest prostitute

8. Cheat on your spouse at a mining conference

9. Secede from Australia

10. Have a cry about your favourite band only touring the eastern states

Broome

Languishing in northern WA, the most forgotten part of the most forgotten state, Broome is an ideal destination if you have committed a terrible crime and need to hide out somewhere where the locals have the natural curiosity of a dead echidna. Popular activities in Broome include committing welfare fraud, hosing condoms off boats and getting arrested for interfering with a camel. The town's official sport is Red Can Green Can, a simple game otherwise known as 'competitive alcoholism'.

Broome is famous for having beaches that look like a postcard, a neat trick that fools hordes of backpackers and Instagram whores into flocking to the town during the dry season, not realising that the rest of town looks more like the set for a film about a zombie apocalypse. When they reach the beach, they usually find that the sea has retreated a hundred metres, the sand is covered in camels and the only people actually using the water are the coastguard looking for boat people to torpedo. The best strip of sand is Cable Beach, so named because it's the most popular place for locals to lay a cable. Upon leaving, tourists soon find that they have sand and red dust throughout their belongings and ingrained in every bodily crevice, which is probably why the place is called Broome.

Broome's history is entwined with pearl diving, a job so safe and rewarding that it was initially given to enslaved Indigenous people and then whatever immigrant group happened to be on the bottom rung at the time. The town was attacked four times by the Japanese during World War II, but despite the Japs' best efforts it managed to cling on like a stubborn skiddy on the bowl, where it remains—defiantly shit—to this day.

TOWN SLOGAN The Gateway to Nowhere.

DID YOU KNOW? Broome's American sister city is Brush, Colorado.

Kalgoorlie

Ever since the 1890s, Kalgoorlie has harboured a reputation as a notorious desert dump full of criminals and prostitutes who had been cast out of polite society, essentially making Kalgoorlie Australia's Australia. Roving bands of delinquent youth spend their days getting wrecked on goon sacks, huffing solvents outside Kmart and getting run over by bogans in utes. This carnage was captured for posterity in the reality TV series *Kalgoorlie Cops*, in which pissed-up P-platers did burnouts in their dads' HSVs and evaded the local constabulary by driving into lampposts.

The most popular tourist attraction in Kalgoorlie is 'The Super Pit', a massive gouge in the earth dedicated to one of Australia's favourite pastimes: raping the earth for shiny things that can be sold to China. Aside from sitting on the precipice of a big stonking hole, Kalgoorlie's main attraction is a tin shack called the Two-Up School, which teaches Kalgoorlites how to throw a couple of coins in the air. Due to the average intelligence of the local populace, courses last several years.

Nightlife in Kalgoorlie centres around the notorious Hay Street, home to several brothels and even a brothel museum for the more cultured Kalhooligan. The city's classy watering holes are known for their traditional 'skimpies nights', where bikini-clad barmaids serve overpriced beer to male miners in jizz-stained overalls. Unfortunately for the sex-starved inhabitants of Kalgoorlie, most of these skimpies are flashing their norks in an outback backwater because they've been spat out the bottom of the more respectable elements of the sex industry.

'Kalgoorlie' originally meant 'place of the silky pears or bush bananas', but in a misguided rebranding attempt it is now hyphenating its name as Kalgoorlie-Boulder, like your uncle's fourth wife. The town was to be the capital of a proposed new state called 'Auralia', which sounds like someone trying to say 'Australia' with a mouthful of bush bananas. It's fair to say no one is mourning the missed opportunity.

TOWN SLOGAN	The Shit By the Pit!
ALSO KNOWN AS	Kal, Hellgoorlie, Smellgoorlie.

Perth

Everyone knows Perthlings are a proud people, but no one knows of what—and no one cares. Perth is famously one of the most isolated capital cities in the world, complete with the exorbitant flight costs and lack of international entertainment that implies. Western Australia's capital may as well be located on the moon as far as the rest of Australia is concerned. This has resulted in a chronic sense of FOMO and a chip on Perth's collective shoulder, turning the local population into a bunch of whiny, self-entitled snobs. Like a petulant teenager who threatens to run away every time their mum bans them from Fortnite, Perth threatens to secede about once a decade.

Built by convict slaves on a wind-blasted and sun-beaten patch of sand, Perth is famous for its brutal summers, the only benefit being the annual purging of the elderly who fail to make it through another blistering January. The city's sole purpose is as an administrative centre for Western Australia's hole-digging industries. As well as subjecting Perth to the sort of rampant inflation common in shonky South American dictatorships, the mining boom has filled the city with cashed-up FIFOs and associated sex workers, who hang out at Scarborough bars and act all upper class with the money that they earned by shovelling dirt or pissing on people.

Other common Pertherts include planeloads of whingeing Poms and white South African apartheid apologists, and hordes of dole-bludging, drug-addicted bogans who tend to live in suburbs like

Armadale. When they're not getting in fights at the traino, Perth residents enjoy weekend trips to Bali where they can lose 65 per cent of their skin in a scooter accident, or excursions to Rottnest Island where the only form of entertainment is punting endangered marsupials into the sea. Closer to home are a number of beaches that are popular locations for being eaten by a shark, Perth residents being some of the tastiest people on the planet.

TOWN SLOGAN Perthetic.

MOST FAMOUS PERSON That loveable larrikin Rolf Harris.

Fremantle

Fremantle is known by a raft of different names, depending on whom you ask. To locals it's 'Freo', as its resident meatheads are unable to process more than two syllables at a time. To its traditional owners it's 'Walyalup', or 'the place of crying', as one look at the place is enough to make even the staunchest bogan burst into tears faster than Steve Smith at a press conference. To anyone else it's 'Fremongrel', 'Feralmantle' or 'that horrible place near Perth'.

Fremantle has a long history of hosting deadshits of various descriptions. The city was named after Charles Fremantle, a British naval officer and accused child rapist. It was later home to ruthless American pirate Bully Hayes (notorious for his crimes against humanity) and former AC/DC frontman Bon Scott (notorious for his crimes against music). The city celebrates Scott with a bronze statue, around which bogans congregate to pay tribute to their hero by drinking themselves into a paralytic state and urinating on his likeness. Other 'Freakmantle' inhabitants include smelly hippies, drug-addled beggars and vicious thugs who flood the central city at the first sign of dusk.

Fremantle's AFL team is called the Dockers, which is gay slang for a sex act far too filthy to describe. Appropriately, the team is headquartered at Cockburn. Despite representing Fremantle, the Dockers could not bring themselves to set foot there, instead playing their home games in Perth.

Tourist activities in Fremantle include visiting a plethora of old prisons, swimming at a windswept beach in front of copious cranes and stacks of rusty shipping containers, or getting mugged by a meth-head.

ALSO KNOWN AS Freo, the People's Republic of Fremantle, Fremuntle, Fremongrel, Feralmantle, Freakmantle.

Mandurah

Mandurah is renowned for its crabs, but it's not just the crustaceans getting cooked—the seaside shitter is also Australia's hard drugs capital, a full-tit meth fest sporting more ice than a polar bear's balls. Popular pastimes include sparking up the glass barbie and fist-fighting in the street, firing up the rock wok and manhandling a crab, or hooning up a canal in a speedboat after shooting the crystal pistol. New York may call itself 'the City that Never Sleeps' but there's even less sleep happening in Methdurah.

In addition to an avalanche of ice, Mandurah has been beset by an inundation of the elderly who have moved in en masse, attracted by the lack of nightlife and immigrants and the hour-long train journey to anywhere resembling civilisation. The coffin-dodger community are quickly claiming Mandurah as their own private retirement village, driving up property prices to the point where Mandurah has been rated as Australia's most unaffordable city. Fortunately, this has little effect on its resident crack-addled crabbers as they spend all their money on meth anyway.

The most popular event on the Mandurah calendar is the city's annual Crab Fest. Highlights include injecting crabs with meth and making them race, injecting crabs with meth and making them fight, and a dress-up competition where punters compete to create the most lifelike pubic louse costume.

FAN MAIL

Immature bunch of complete wankers who wouldnt
know a good thing if it pissed on your foot. Go
get a real job fucktards. **(VIC MUSPRATT, BROOME)**

You have won tool and fuckwit of the year
tosser. **(SHANE GRAVY, KALGOORLIE)**

Who the fuck is this ARSOLE. Come over to Perth and i'll
punch your fucking lights out. **('BUTCH' QUIGLEY, PERTH)**

Don't put shit on my home town. you need
a ass woopin. **(STEVE CLENCH, MANDURAH)**

Tuggabugga

Tuggabugga is known mainly for three things: incest, religious extremism and toxic industrial waste, making it more Australian than a kangaroo doing it up the wrong 'un while singing 'Flame Trees' and doing a shoey of Tooheys New. Filled with three-legged dogs, petrol-sniffing toddlers and inbred dole bludgers, this is a place so backwards that babies eat dingoes.

The town was founded by a radical sect of Anglicans after they were ostracised from society when their leader wrote a new version of the Bible that emphasised itchy undergarments and camel marriage. It was then populated by convicts who were exiled from convict colonies for reoffending, making Tuggabugga the country's only convict colony convict colony. The small community has bred exclusively within itself for generations, resulting in a gene pool so shallow that it's more of a gene puddle.

Tuggabugga is home to Australia's largest open-cast glitter mine (known locally as 'the Old Axe Wound'), responsible for producing 50 per cent of the world's glitter. Glitter from the mine has been used to make a range of products, from the disco balls in the Sydney Opera House to Shane Warne's personal supply of zinc to all the titty glitter that gave the Gold Coast its 'Glitter Strip' nickname. An unfortunate side effect of this once prosperous industry, Tuggabugga is now covered in a thin layer of shiny shit so toxic that the townsfolk wish it was asbestos. Many residents are afflicted with sparkly lung, a fatal disease that sees sufferers coughing up delightful rainbows of metastasised lung tissue.

Aside from the glitter mine, Tuggabugga's main tourist attractions are the Big Dingleberry and the Ear Wax Museum, both conveniently located on the town's main (and only) road. Another favourite feature is the statue of local celebrity Graeme, Australia's first donkey mayor, who held office for a staggering 30 years barring a six-month suspension for corruption after he ate several sensitive documents.

Despite its inhabitants, atmosphere and distinct smell, Tuggabugga's sparkly facade and over three attractions make it well worth a trip. In fact, it's probably the only town in this book worth visiting.

INDEX

Allen & Unwin
83 Alexander Street
Crows Nest NSW 2065
Australia
Phone: (61 2) 8425 0100
Email: info@allenandunwin.com
Web: www.allenandunwin.com

A catalogue record for this book is available from the National Library of Australia

ISBN 978 1 98854 724 4

Set in 10.5/14.5 Sofia Pro Light by Kate Barraclough
Printed in China by C & C Offset Printing Co. Ltd

10 9 8 7 6 5